What's So Funny?

(A Foreign Student's Introduction to American Humor)

by

Elizabeth Claire

Pictures by eluki bes shahar

Eardley Publications, P.O. Box 281
Rochelle Park, NJ 07662

ISBN 0-937630-01-2

Eardley Publications, P.O. Box 281
Rochelle Park, N.J. 07662

For my Grandmother
Elizabeth Klimek,
who at the age of 94
still likes nothing better
than to hear or tell a good joke.

Ha ha, Babka,
Ja ta lubim.

About the Author

Elizabeth Claire graduated magna cum laude from the City College of New York, and received her Master's Degree in Teaching English as a Second Language through the Experienced Teacher Fellowship Program at New York University in 1968. She has taught English as a Second Language for the past eighteen years to students of all ages, from kindergarten to senior citizen. She is currently an ESL specialist with the Fort Lee Public Schools in New Jersey.

Other works by Elizabeth Claire:

HI!: English for Children in American Schools, (Minerva Books, Ltd.)

A Foreign Student's Guide to Dangerous English (Eardley, $5.95)

Just-A-Minute, a language-learning game (Eardley, $8.95)

ACKNOWLEDGEMENTS

This book could not have been produced in its current form without the assistance of many people. I owe a great debt of thanks to the following:

To Anna Eardley, for being my mother; to Jimmy and Jon Simms--Jimmy for listening to my plans and problems while cooking his own meals, and Jon for climbing Mount Katahdin with a fully outfitted canoe; to Dr. Reinhold Aman, editor of Maledicta Press, and Roger Olsen, editor of Alemany Press for reading early versions of the manuscript and giving encouragement and advice; to Frank Jacobs, of MAD magazine for insights into the nature of humor; to Richard Buehler, Agnes Zongora, Bernie Gould, Warren Murphy, Nela Alvarez, Janet Cuccinelli, Seth Cohen, and Joy Norin, all for encouragement and advice along the way; to the Writers' Anonymous Group of Northern New Jersey Mensa (Sharon Bailly, George Victor, John O'Conner, Jonathan Steele, Frank Smead, Gene Cackson, Tom Napier, and Barbara Wheeler), for critical feedback on the manuscript; to Bea Pfeffer, Leo Marrazzo, Allen Neuner, Wendy Sailer, Diane Hope-Friedel, Cathy Brandt, Ophelia Bailly, Charles Martin, Art Davis and many others for scouring the countryside for some really funny jokes.

I also want to thank the following new speakers of English for their helpful detailed line-by-line analysis of, and commentary on the readability of this work:

Kraisorn and Mercedes Charoen, Chantha Chum, Fukiko Shinohara, Yumiko Mabashi, Dolores Cuevos, and Boris Rizberg.

TO THE TEACHER

What's So Funny? is a unique, many-angled approach to helping non-native English speakers break through the cultural and linguistic barriers to American humor. It was designed for intermediate and advanced college conversation classes for foreign students in the United States. It may also be used in high school ESL and adult education programs, and in classes abroad. Foreign businesspeople, immigrants, and visitors to the country can enjoy and benefit from the book without formal instruction.

Selections are short; potentially troublesome words are boldfaced and marked with an asterisk. These words are defined in easy English at the back of the book. Self-checking vocabulary and idiom exercises mean greater student independence in preparing each lesson. Insights into American ways of thinking and cultural stereotypes will set the stage for discussions of contrasts with the students' own cultural stereotypes.

The nature of the subject--humor--insures enthusiastic student involvement in in-class and, more importantly, out-of-class conversations. No other subject generates such lively participation, covering so many different linguistic skills.

Chapters One through Five provide the framework and vocabulary for discussing further jokes. The explanation of the nature of stereotypes in Chapters Four and Five should be well understood by students to avoid misinterpretations of stereotypes described later in the book.

After the students have read and discussed the first five chapters, you may wish to assign the reading of Chapter Sixteen--"How to Tell a Joke." The other chapters may be taken in any order, depending on the time and interests of the class. Remember that glossed words are indicated by an asterisk only the first time they are cited, however, so that a straight progression through the book is preferable, at least for less-advanced students who will need the vocabulary support.

Some suggestions for instruction:

For intermediate classes:

If you have a good supply of your own jokes, you might want to start each class with a joke relevant to the chapter to be discussed. Or you can prepare for each reading assignment by introducing one of the discussion questions from the end of the chapter. After several minutes of give-and-take, announce the title of the chapter to be read for homework, or in class. On the board, write the words you expect will be troublesome to your students. Elicit meanings and have students use the words in sentences if they can. (You might assign different students to look up different words in the glossary, so that all can participate in volunteering information.) When the vocabulary has been prepared, assign the reading of the chapter.

On the following day, review the vocabulary and idiom exercises; ask students if they had any difficulties with the readings. Select essential or difficult paragraphs to be read aloud in class. Which jokes did they like the most? Which jokes were not funny to them? Use the discussion questions to stimulate student interaction. If your class is large, you might want to divide the students into groups of four or five, or let the students work in pairs, so all students will have an opportunity to give their opinions and tell jokes in a non-threatening situation. Appoint a leader (or let each group select its own leader) to keep the discussions going. Students should be encouraged to share jokes they have heard, or jokes from their own countries on the topic under discussion.

After the small group discussion, the group members or leaders might report any difficulties, controversies, or funny stories to the larger group.

Advanced students will need less help with vocabulary and the literal meanings of the readings and jokes. They may still need explanations and guidance regarding the background information and American stereotypes. You may assign chapters as outside readings, and use the discussion questions as a point of departure for classroom interaction.

Applications:

Assign students to watch a currently popular TV situation comedy and report to the class on the success or difficulty of understanding the humor. You might tape an episode either on tape recorder or video recorder to play back as many times as necessary. Tapes of portions of some TV variety shows, the Tonight Show, Saturday Night Live, etc., will bring current trends and topics of humor into the classroom. Discuss the stereotypes depicted, types of humor used, butts of the jokes, and word plays utilized.

Have students bring in cartoons and comic strips for a class bulletin board of humor. Some comic strips illustrate the Battle of the Sexes, some the difficulties of children, the stresses of adolescence, the tensions of school, dealing with other people, or the annoyances of army life, the business world or specific occupations, or the ironies of the world situation. If the students have access to cartoons and comics in their own language newpapers, have them write translations of the captions and share them with the class.

Have students read a column written by current American humorists such as Erma Bombeck, Art Buchwald or Russell Baker. Encourage the students to bring in jokes they have heard, to clip cartoons for a class humor collection or bulletin board.

Encourage your joke tellers to be sensitive to the racial, sexual, personal and ethnic taboos in joke-telling in the class. We have selected jokes that are representative of various themes in American humor, and have noted where some jokes might be considered funny by one group and not by another group. We have made every effort to treat political, religious and ethnic jokes as tactfully as possible.

Although we have drawn stereotypes of various occupational groups and family relationships, we have strictly avoided painting specific ethnic stereotypes that underly many of the jokes the students may hear elsewhere. It is left to the teacher to use his or her own discretion in dealing with this issue with any particular class. Jokes of a sexual or scatological nature do not appear at all in this volume.

The funny bone is a very individual thing. Encourage the students to state when they find a joke offensive. Use these revelations to guide discussion and support of the dignity of each student and each culture.

TABLE OF CONTENTS

1

TO THE STUDENT

The ability to laugh is one of Nature's greatest gifts. Laughter can make us forget our problems or give us new courage to face them. It can cheer us when we are sad, and heal us when we are sick. Laughing makes learning easier. Laughing together turns strangers into friends.

We all need laughter to help us **cope*** with the difficulties of life and the troubles of the world. For a newcomer in a foreign land, laughter is especially welcome. A sense of humor is a great help in dealing with the stress of living in a new country and speaking a new language.

This book was written to help you begin to understand the American sense of humor. We had a lot of fun writing it. We hope you have fun reading it.

Elizabeth Claire

* There is a glossary of 400 words at the end of the book. Words and phrases that are marked with a star will be found there.

<> Jokes will be marked with this symbol.

2

CHAPTER ONE: What's So Funny?

You are at a party, in a room full of Americans, and you are having fun. Your English has been improving steadily and you now feel comfortable and confident on any general subject of conversation.

Then someone begins to tell a joke.

"Did you hear the one about the three sisters?" asks the young man in the arm chair by the window. Everyone's attention turns to him. You listen too, as he begins. The joke is not difficult to follow. You understand every word. But suddenly, the whole group of people bursts out laughing.

<u>You</u> are still waiting for the end of the joke. Was that last

3

sentence the **punch line***? Did it go **right over your head?***

You wish you **had the nerve*** to ask someone to explain, but in a moment, a man on the sofa says,

"That reminds me about the drunk who went to a bar and..." You listen extra carefully this time, but the same thing happens again. Everyone is laughing but you. So you laugh politely too. But you wish you understood what the **point*** of the joke was.

After a while you decide to tell a funny story of your own. It is a joke many people have enjoyed in your own country. When you **deliver the punch line*** you feel a great sense of satisfaction and wait for your friends to laugh. They just look at you, puzzled, and **chuckle*** politely.

What went wrong?

While students learning English in America frequently find much to laugh at with their new American friends, the structured humor of jokes remains very difficult to understand. There are so many ways to miss the point of a joke.

In ordinary conversation, you can miss ten or twenty percent of what the speaker is saying, and you still have a pretty good chance of getting the full meaning. In something as brief as a joke, missing one **key*** word can prevent understanding.

There may be a **play on words***. Here a certain word is deliberately used because it has more than one meaning. If you don't know the double meaning of the word, you will not **get the point***.

Background information may be necessary to understand a joke. You may not know certain current events, customs, history, and personalities commonly known to Americans.

Americans hold **stereotypes*** of people in certain occupations, **ethnic groups***, or relationships. These may not be familiar to you and you probably hold different stereotypes.

Certain subjects often cause laughter among Americans whereas those subjects may not be laughed at in your culture. It is quite permissable (and very common) for an American to laugh in public at jokes about the President, for example, though

4

it may be **taboo*** to laugh publicly at the king or queen, or emperor in some countries.

A foreign student needs help with all of these difficulties, and we hope that this little book will give you a good beginning. We would like to help you increase your vocabulary and gain some cultural insights into American ways of thinking. We hope we can **tickle your funny bone*** while you are learning!

What is laughter?

Scientists have been studying laughter for many years. They have already discovered some of the **neurological*** and biological reasons for laughter.

A human baby begins to smile during its second month. This is a **reflex*** in reaction to pleasure, and sometimes to pain. The baby is able to burst into laughter two months later. Laughter is not always in response to pleasure. **Irritations*** such as **tickling*** cause laughter. Fear, worry, shame, embarrassment and other **tensions*** may also cause laughter.

Our complex emotions and good memories make us capable of psychological **conflicts***. The conflicts create tensions within us. Our daily lives may also bring fear, embarrassment, **guilt***, **resentment***, and anger.

Laughter is a **safety valve*** that relieves these pressures and tensions. In heavy laughter, the muscles of the face and chest **contract*** **convulsively***. Our heart rate speeds up. Our breathing and **circulation*** speed up, too. After the laughter, our heart rate slows down and our muscles relax. Our brains become more **alert***.

When we laugh, a **hormone*** that **stimulates*** the production of **endorphins*** is released. Endorphins are the body's own natural pain killers. Ten minutes of heavy laughter can give an hour's relief from pain. Laughter really is "the best medicine".

What do Americans laugh at?

In many cases, Americans laugh at exactly the same things people in your country laugh at. There are many jokes which travel around the world, translated into various languages in almost identical form.

5

In places where tensions are similar, similar jokes are popular.

Tensions occur when laws, religions, traditions, or other people **interfere*** with people's needs or desires.

Tensions develop where there is resentment caused by unequal distribution of power, wealth, opportunity, or **material*** and emotional satisfactions.

Tensions increase when there are fears of crime, unemployment, **economic recession***, **epidemics***, war, or other disasters that are out of the individual's control.

Biological differences between people can cause tensions too, because society rewards some qualities and punishes others. People are either male or female, and may be tall or short, lean or fat, intelligent or **dull***, strong or weak, beautiful or ugly, old or young, dark-skinned or light skinned. Interactions between any two people can cause feelings of jealousy, fear, resentment, anger, or anxiety.

As children, we may spill our milk, fail in school, be hurt, be insulted, or be spanked for some wrongdoing. Later, we may lose our jobs, our house may burn down, our marriages may be unhappy. We may lose at golf, lose our hair, lose our money, and eventually, lose our lives. We spend a lot of energy trying to avoid these disasters. Our daily lives are filled with time limits, speed limits, standing in line, wrong numbers, **indigestion***, misunderstandings, and many other stresses.

Seeing the funny side of these misfortunes can keep us from being **overwhelmed*** by them.

In jokes, we may see these misfortunes and disasters happen to other, imaginary people. We laugh and release tension. It is a relief when <u>someone else</u> is clumsier, dumber, unluckier, or poorer than we are. If <u>someone else</u> slips on a banana peel, we may laugh, because it isn't us. (The idea is even funnier if the victim is disliked.)

Humor **at the expense of*** one group (such as politicians or mothers-in-law) may be an attempt at keeping that group "**in line**"*. People do not like to have their behavior **ridiculed.*** As a result, some may change their behavior so they will not be laughed at. In this way, humor is used as a very powerful weapon. Even if the ridiculed people do not change their

behavior, anger towards them is released in a socially acceptable way.

Often a person will tell jokes at his own expense in order to lower the anxiety or resentment that others might feel. Laughter can **smooth over*** difficulties between groups of people. For example, a lawyer might tell a joke about lawyers when he is talking to an audience of non-lawyers.

Sometimes it's hard for a foreign student to see why an American thinks something is funny.

The foreign student may not experience tension in a similar situation. For example, in America, men are considered more attractive if they have a full head of hair. However, many men lose their hair or fear losing it. As a result there are many jokes about **baldness.*** Asian men generally do not become bald. There is no anxiety about losing one's hair or attractiveness in this area, so there will be fewer jokes in Japan, China, or Korea about baldness. In a culture where a bald head is considered a sign of **wisdom***, or where men regularly shave their heads, there will also be no reason for jokes about baldness.

Goethe, the famous German writer, said that people show their character most clearly in what they find laughable. Even in one society, there are many different opinions as to what is funny. We are influenced by our education, our social class, our **ethnic background***, religion, sex, job, age, and our life experiences.

Exercises

I Vocabulary   Match these definitions with the words and idioms* from this chapter:

1. good judgement, intelligence____   A. survive

2. remain alive ____   B. wisdom

3. to fail to understand____   C. chuckle

4. the last line of a joke____   D. indigestion

5. having to do with nerves____   E. resentment

6. stomach ache____   F. miss the point

7. having no hair____   G. key

8. anger____   H. endorphin

9. a natural pain killer____   I. punch line

10. a time of unemployment____   J. bald

11. spread of disease____   K. recession

12. laugh softly____   L. epidemic

13. Essential part____   M. neurological

II How well did you read?

Write TRUE or FALSE on the line after the sentence.

1. There are many ways to miss the point of a joke.

_____

2. If you miss ten or twenty percent of a joke, you can still get the full meaning. _____

3. Irritations such as tickling can cause laughter. _____

9

4. Tension may be caused by fear, resentment, anger, and differences between people. _____

5. Laughter is a safety valve that releases pressure and tensions. _____

6. During heavy laughter, our heart rate slows down. _____

7. Laughter helps us stay healthy. _____

8. Humor can be a powerful social force. _____

9. People generally enjoy being ridiculed. _____

10. In America, a bald head is considered a sign of wisdom and attractiveness. _____

III Discussion

1. Have you had difficulty understanding American jokes? Have you told a joke that no one understood?

2. What are some of the reasons a foreign student may fail to understand a joke in English?

3. Can you think of some of the special tensions a newcomer to the U.S. experiences?

4. Are jokes about your president or other political leaders common in your country?

5. What social or political tensions can you describe in your country?

6. Are there jokes about baldness in your country?

CHAPTER TWO: The Structure of a Joke

A joke has a point.

The point is the important, essential or primary element that causes the laughter.

A joke or story may make people laugh when it contains one or more of the following elements:

> surprise
> embarrassment
> **illogic***
> **exaggeration***

We may laugh if the joke does one or more of the following:

1. It breaks social or sexual **taboos***.

2. Other people or groups are made to look **inferior***, making the teller and listener feel **superior**.

3. People in **authority***, or people who are resented, are made to appear foolish.

4. Accidents, pain, disaster, shame, or other misfortunes happen to someone else.

5. Things are taken out of their normal order or location.

6. Events are connected in unexpected ways.

In addition to having a point, many jokes also have a "butt"*. This is the object, person, or group of people that is being made fun of. The "butt" is the object of resentment, jealousy, anger, fear, guilt, or other anxiety. Sometimes the listener is the butt of the joke. The teller of the joke may make himself the butt.

In a joke, we punish the butt in some way. We make the butts appear silly, stupid, **stingy***, cruel, dishonest, **deceitful***, selfish, dirty, uneducated, lazy, **greedy***, ridiculous, dangerous or inferior. We fool them, embarrass them, hurt them or even kill them in a joke. No blood is spilled, so we can even get **away with murder***.

Most people do not analyze jokes in this way. They just know that some jokes are funny and some are not. They enjoy hearing and telling the ones that make them and other people laugh.

The following are typical "butts" of humor in America. How many are butts of humor in your country?

Men, women, marriage, husbands, wives, mothers-in-law, parents, children, younger brothers and sisters, neighbors.

School, teachers, smart students, stupid students.

People in authority: policemen, bosses, landlords, congressmen, the President, politics, politicians.

Rich people, movie stars, lawyers.

Work, workers, secretaries, lazy people, unemployment.

Religion, religious leaders.

Doctors and psychiatrists and their patients.

National and ethnic groups, foreigners, foreign accents.

City people, farmers, tourists, people from other regions of the country.

Salesmen, customers, restaurant food, waiters, barbers, dogs and dog owners.

Physical differences: people who are fat, skinny, bald, deaf, have big noses, etc., or are **handicapped***.

Modern civilization: inventions, computers, modern art, airplane travel, world tensions, Communism,

12

crime, fears, pollution, taxes, high prices, current news items.

Humor that is based on **hostility*** is not equally funny to everyone. The teller of a joke should be aware that a joke about wives may be funny to men but not to women. Republicans may enjoy a political joke that Democrats will find unfunny. Jokes about ethnic groups will amuse some people, but offend others.

Jokes often come "in threes". When listeners hear "Three drunks went to heaven and . . ." they know that they can expect something funny to happen to the drunks. Usually, the first two characters will say, do, or experience something similar. The third will provide the **twist***.

Jokes may be told in the past tense, but very often the present tense is used. As in other oral story telling, the use of the present tense helps include the listener in the story. Some jokes may be told either way.

The beginning of a joke is the **build up.*** The beginning builds up an expectation, or creates tension.

The end of the joke is called the **"punch line*."** The punch line delivers the "punch"--the surprise, or the relief from the tension.

Let's take a simple joke and analyze it:

<> Did you hear about the man who had three wives? Two of them died from eating poisonous mushrooms. The third one died of a **fractured* skull***. . . She wouldn't eat the poisonous mushrooms.

Did you hear about the man who had three wives? This introduction gets the listener's attention. It is not announced as a joke, so the listener might even think it is a news item. With divorce and remarriage so common in America, however, three wives does not sound so unusual, unless the man had all three wives at the same time. We want to find out.

Two of them died from eating poisonous mushrooms. Now we know that

13

14

the man did not get divorced, but lost his wives through death. Talking about death creates tension. Any of us may lose a spouse. We feel sympathy for the man; but at the same time, we wonder at the **coincidence*** that two of his wives should both be so careless as to eat poisonous mushrooms. Gullible listeners may still feel they are being told a true story or item from the newspaper.

(As background information, it is necessary to know that eating poisonous mushrooms is not an unusual cause of death in the United States. There are many people who pick wild mushrooms. It is difficult to distinguish the **edible*** varieties from the poisonous ones.)

The third one died of a fractured skull. The listener is curious. Did she have an accident? Did she fall? Perhaps there is still more sympathy for the man who has now lost three wives.

. . . The **pause*** before the punch line. This gives the listeners enough time to think about and fully understand what we have heard so far, and build up an expectation. We may mentally begin to formulate some explanation for the strange **sequence*** of events. The pause must not be too long, however.

She wouldn't eat the poisonous mushrooms. Now we know that the man has murdered his own wives! And that this was not a true story after all, but merely a joke.

This joke will be funny to many Americans, both men and women. **Underlying*** (perhaps unconscious) tensions that are released by the punch line are:

A fear of death.
Fears of marriage, felt by a single person.
Resentment of a wife, felt by a husband.
Fear of a husband, felt by a wife.

We may all have secret or unconscious angry impulses, which we do not act out. In this joke, angry impulses are expressed in an exaggerated way: murder, not of just one wife, but three.

There are people who will think this joke is not funny at all. Young people, idealistic people, and happily married people may not laugh at it. This is not that they do not have a sense of humor. Since they do not feel tension in these areas, they will not have experienced the tension release that **triggers*** laughter.

15

Exercises

I Vocabulary   Choose the correct word from the list to complete the sentences:

inferior	butt	punch line	pause
hostility	stingy	deceitful	
point	authority	greedy	

1. The _____ of a joke is the important, essential, or primary element that causes laughter.

2. The _____ of a joke is the object, person, or group of people that is being made fun of.

3. The President, policemen, and teachers are examples of people in _____.

4. The part of the joke that makes us laugh is the _____.

5. A person might feel _____ to a boss, movie star, or a very wealthy person.

6. People who do not like to spend money or share things, even with their families, may be called _____.

7. People who try to get more than their fair share of money or food may be called _____.

8. A person who tells lies is _____.

9. Feeling or showing anger is called _____.

10. A short rest or waiting period is a _____.

II Discussion

1. What are some elements of a joke that can make people laugh?

2. What are some common butts of humor in your country?

3. What was your reaction to the man who poisoned his wives with the mushrooms?

CHAPTER THREE: Children's Humor

Children are just beginning to understand the world around them. So much is new to them that they often burst into laughter from pure surprise. A five-year-old will delight his elders with his laughter at the first sight of an elephant, or Jack o'lantern or snowman. Things out of their usual order or place cause youngsters of 5, 6 and 7 to laugh uproariously*. A picture of a dog smoking a cigar, a fish in a bird's nest, or a man rowing a boat up a mountain will bring squeals of laughter.

Riddles

One of the earliest forms of humor a child learns (around age 6) is the riddle. A riddle is a question with a "trick" answer.

A riddle often depends on word play for its surprise answer. By using a word with a double meaning, the listener is tricked into a wrong answer or cannot guess the correct answer. Children discovering the joys of playing with words will ask riddles with never-ending enthusiasm*. They are not aware that most of their riddles are "as old as the hills" and that adults have heard them a hundred times. If six-year-old Johnnie asks you if you want to hear some riddles, it may be a good idea to set a time limit in advance.

Read over this vocabulary list to help prepare you for the children's riddles that follow.

eye: The hole in a sewing needle.

mouth: The place where a river flows into the ocean.

face: The front of a clock.

horn: 1. An instrument for making music or noise; a car has a horn to warn others to get out of the way. 2. The bony growth on a cow's or goat's head.

17

Now can you **"get*"** these children's riddles?

  1. Question: What has an eye but cannot see? **Give up*?**
     Answer: A needle.

  2. Q: What has hands and a face, but cannot talk?
     A: A clock.

  3. Q: What has a mouth but cannot talk?
     A: A river.

  4. Q: What has only one horn and gives milk?
     A: A milk truck.

  5. Q: Why does a cow wear a bell?
     A: Because its horns don't work.

There are other kinds of word plays. Some words may function as more than one part of speech. A sentence with such words is **ambiguous.*** It can be understood in two different ways.

  fly = noun. A small insect. There are flies on the window.

  fly = verb. Travel through the air. An airplane flies.

  6. Q: What has four wheels and flies?

(We are tricked into thinking the question means, "What has four wheels and can fly?" We try to think of some form of transportation--an airplane with four wheels, a helicopter, etc.

But the answer is a surprise!

What has four wheels and flies? A garbage truck. We can now see that the question really meant, "What has four wheels and also has flies.")

  7. Q: What is the best way to keep fish from smelling?

(We may think this question means How can we keep the

18

fish from having a bad **odor***?) We guess, "wash it with lemon juice," "cook it in wine", etc.

The answer shows us we were mistaken in our thinking.)

7. Q: What is the best way to keep fish from smelling? Cut off their noses!

(Then they cannot notice the odors around them.)

8. Q: Why did my little brother tiptoe past the medicine cabinet?
A: He didn't want to wake the sleeping pills.

(Sleeping pills = pills that help people fall asleep. The little brother thinks that sleeping pills are pills that are sleeping.)

see verb. 1. Notice with the eyes. 2. Understand.

saw 1. verb. The past form of "see". 2. noun. A tool used for cutting wood.

<> "Oh, I see," said the blind carpenter, as he picked up his hammer and saw.

Other riddles are based on **paradoxes***. See if you can match the correct answers to the following riddles.

ANSWERS:

A. nine cents   B.the fence
C. the sidewalk   D. the letter M
E. an egg   F. a tea pot
G. a sponge   H. finding half a worm

1. What goes up in the air white and comes down yellow and white?____

2. What goes up to the door, but never goes in?____

3. I am once in every minute, twice in every moment, but never in a thousand years.____

4. What is worse than finding a worm in an apple?____

19

5. What runs all around the yard but never moves?___

6. What is full of holes but yet holds water?___

7. What starts with a T, ends with a T, and is full of T?___

8. What's the difference between an old penny and a new dime?___

> Q: What do they call watermelons in Louisiana?
> A: Watermelons.

The surprise here is that there is no trick, when we expected one.

> Ed: What's the difference between a loaf of bread and a bunch of bananas?
> Ned: I don't know.
> Ed: You'd be a fine one to send to the store for a loaf of bread!

(The teller has tricked the listener. It sounded like a riddle, but it wasn't. By saying I don't know, the listener has shown he is not very smart!)

The pecking order*

On a farm, observers of animals have noted that chickens and other animals have a "pecking order". The **dominant*** chicken in the flock may **peck** at all the others. The second dominant chicken may peck at all the others except the most dominant one. The third may peck at all under it. The **lowest-ranking*** chicken gets pecked at by all the others.

Human society has its "pecking order", too. Children are often at the bottom of this pecking order.

A boss loses an important contract worth many thousands of dollars. He is angry and **yells*** at his workers. The workers cannot yell back at their bosses for fear of losing their jobs. They go home and yell at their wives. The wife may yell at a child, who in turn yells at a younger child. The younger child **takes** it **out on*** the dog.

It is not comfortable to be yelled at or pecked at. Often telling jokes about those above or below one in the pecking order

20

can relieve the tension of being **pushed around***. Children's humor is full of jokes causing embarrassment or misfortune to occur to the people in power in their lives.

Children may be jealous of their younger brothers and sisters. They have to take orders from older children, parents and other relatives. Jokes about these relatives help children express their resentment.

School is a place of great anxiety for many children. Teachers, tests, homework, report cards, smarter children, and stupid children are the butts of many children's jokes.

Exercises

I Can you identify the butts in these jokes?

<> Aunt Martha: Well, Timmy, how do you like school?
Timmy: Closed!

<> Aunt Martha: And what are you going to give your baby brother for Christmas this year?
Timmy: I don't know. Last year I gave him the **measles***.

<> Mother: Tommy, why did you put a frog in your little sister's bed?
Tommy: Because I couldn't find a mouse.

(Tommy would have put a mouse in the bed if he had found one. He thinks it is a natural thing to put scary things in the bed of someone you hate.)

<> Mother: Tommy, there were two pieces of pie in the cupboard this morning and now there is only one. Can you explain that?
Tommy: It was so dark, I didn't see the other

22

piece.

<> Teacher: Billy, if you had two dollars in one pocket and five dollars in another, what would you have?

Billy: Someone else's pants, Ma'm.

<> Father: Look at all these bills! Everything is **going up***! Gas, telephone, food, clothes, doctor bills...I'd be happy if just one thing went down.

Junior: OK, **Pop***. Now is a good time to look at my report card.

<>Father: This report card says that you failed everything except geography. Can you explain that?

Kid: Sure. I don't take geography.

<> Susie: Mommy! Charlie broke my doll!

Mother: That's too bad, dear. How did he do it?

Susie: I hit him over the head with it.

<> Frantic mother: Doctor, Come at once! Our baby has swallowed a ball-point pen!

Doctor: I'll be right there. What are you doing in the meantime?

Mother: We're using a pencil.

<> Babysitter: While you were out, little Annie ate a **cockroach***. But don't worry about it. I made her swallow some roach poison.

<> Teacher: What is the difference between electricity and lightning?

Student: We don't have to pay for lightning.

<>Timmy: Let's play school.

Jimmy: OK. Let's play I'm absent.

<> Teacher: Did your father help you with this homework problem?
Pupil: No, I got it wrong by myself.

<> Little Timmy was visiting his grandfather. In the morning, Grandpa decided to make a big pot of oatmeal. He put some oatmeal into a bowl for Timmy. "Do you like sugar?" Grandpa asked.
"Yes," said Timmy.
So Grandpa put sugar on the oatmeal. "Do you like milk?"
"Yes," said Timmy.
So Grandpa put some milk on the oatmeal. "Do you like butter?"
"Yes," said Timmy.
So Grandpa put some butter on the oatmeal. Then he placed the bowl of oatmeal in front of Timmy.
"YUKK!" said Timmy.
"What's the matter? I asked you if you liked sugar, milk, and butter and you said yes, so I put them on," said Grandpa, getting angry.
"You didn't ask me if I like oatmeal," said Timmy.

II Vocabulary   Choose the best answer:

1. A cockroach is a (an) _____

    a. kind of riddle
    b. insect
    c. paradox

2. An ambiguous sentence _____

    a. has more than one meaning
    b. is uproariously funny
    c. contains the butt of the joke

3. A taboo is _____

    a. something forbidden
    b. a trick answer to a riddle
    c. a musical instrument

4. Teachers, parents, policemen and bosses are _____

      a. at the bottom of the pecking order
      b. ethnic groups
      c. authority figures

5. The measles are a kind of ____

      a. disease
      b. riddle
      c. punch line

6. "Everything is going up" means that _____

      a. things are flying.
      b. things are difficult to understand.
      c. prices are increasing.

7. If a person is enthusiastic, he or she is ____

      a. unaware
      b. interested and excited
      c. dominant

8. The hole in a sewing needle is the ___

      a. mouth
      b. horn
      c. eye

III Discussion

1. Which of the jokes were funny to you?

2. Which jokes were not funny to you?

3. Give some examples of children's riddles from your country. What happens to the "word play" when your translate the riddle?

4. Do children freely tell jokes about teachers and parents in your country?

5. Try telling one of these jokes in front of a mirror. Then tell it to someone. Describe the reactions of the listeners.

CHAPTER FOUR: What Is a Stereotype*?

A stereotype is an over-simplified belief or opinion about groups of people. Stereotypes are <u>not</u> always true. They may even be almost completely false.

Examples of stereotypes: "Italians are very emotional." "New Yorkers are always in a hurry." "Doctors are rich." "Politicians are **crooks***." "Jews are intelligent." "Fat people are **jolly***."

It <u>is</u> true that <u>some</u> Italians are very emotional, <u>some</u> New Yorkers <u>are</u> in a hurry much of the time, <u>some</u> doctors are rich, <u>some</u> politicians are crooks, <u>some</u> Jews are <u>intelligent</u>, and <u>some</u> fat people are jolly.

<u>But "some" does not mean "all"</u>. <u>"Some" does not even mean most</u>.

People notice the behavior or characteristics of outstanding* members of a group. They then think that other members of the group (whom they have <u>not</u> met or read about) have the same behavior or characteristics. This lazy thinking is called stereotyping.

Stereotyped attitudes are spread in a culture through newspapers, movies, TV, literature, textbooks, and jokes as well as through personal contact.

Stereotypes may be positive or negative. Let's look at the stereotypes Americans hold of the profession of doctor.

Positive stereotype: Doctors are intelligent, respected, useful members of the community. Doctors are rich. A doctor would make a good **catch*** as a husband. You should trust your doctor.

Negative stereotype: Doctors' **fees*** are too high. Doctors make many mistakes in **diagnosis*** and recommend unecessary operations. A doctor would rather make money than help his patients. Doctors like to keep patients waiting.

Many jokes depend on stereotypes. You will read about the stereotyped attitudes Americans have about many different groups of people. Understanding the stereotypes will help you see why Americans laugh at certain jokes.

Let's look at some jokes based on a common American stereotype: the mother-in-law. She is perhaps the most **maligned*** person in the history of American humor.

The stereotype of the mother-in-law is that she is powerful, **manipulative***, **meddlesome***, and talkative. (The mother of the wife is considered worse than the mother of the husband.) She treats her daughter as if she were still a child and never considers that her daughter's husband is "good enough" for her daughter. She **interferes*** in her daughter's marriage, and makes the husband miserable. She comes for long visits, gives unwanted advice and talks endlessly. She makes unreasonable demands for visits and attention.

It is difficult to "let go" of one's children, even when they are grown and married. It is true that some mothers-in-law fit this stereotype. There are other mothers-in-law who have some of the negative qualities mentioned. But in general, most mothers-(and fathers)-in-law help their married children financially, give encouragement, and do not give advice when it is not asked for. They babysit cheerfully and enjoy a good relationship with their children and grandchildren.

In cases where there is a great deal of tension between mothers and sons-in-law, the son-in-law may be the one **in the wrong***. He may be lazy, rude, **sloppy***, and a poor provider. An **insecure*** husband may **resent*** sharing his wife's love. He will **magnify*** his mother-in-law's negative behavior and **minimize*** her positive qualities. It has generally been the males in our culture who create and tell the most jokes. So men tell many jokes about mothers-in-law, while the mothers-in-law tell very few in return.

There are many people who have poor relationships with their wives or their own mothers and feel guilty or fearful about this. The hidden butt in a mother-in-law joke might be one's own mother. Or a joke may be a way of expressing hostility towards one's wife, or all women. In this way, the stereotype about mothers-in-law is **reinforced***.

<> Boy, can my mother-in-law talk. She went to **Miami*** and she came back with her tongue sunburned.

27

<> A hundred thousand years ago, a
cave-woman* yelled to her cave-man husband: "Help!
There's a **saber-toothed tiger*** here! He went into
the cave where my mother is! Do something!"
The cave man **grunted***, "Why should I care
what happens to the tiger?"

(The mother-in-law is so powerful and mean, she will
probably kill the tiger.)

<> A **mule*** had kicked the farmer's mother-in-law in the
head and she died. A huge crowd from miles around **showed
up*** at the **funeral***.
"Your mother-in-law must have been a wonderful person for
so many people to come to her funeral," said the **minister***.
"Oh, they're not here for the funeral," said the farmer.
"They came here to ask to borrow the mule."

Mothers-in-law can **strike back***: This joke illustrates the
childish **ingratitude*** and **lack*** of achievement of a son-in-law:

<> A man was complaining to a **bartender***,
"My mother-in-law has been living with us for years,
and it's driving me crazy."
"Why don't you ask her to move?
"I'd love to, but I can't. It's her house."

Humor about mothers-in-law has several results.
People who resent their mothers-in-law can enjoy jokes about
them, and thus **get rid of*** some hostility. Humor can call
attention to unwanted behavior and cause people to change it.
Mothers-in-law may try to be different from the mothers-in-law in
the jokes.

Exercises

I Vocabulary

Match the best definition to the following words:

1. stereotype _____
2. meddlesome _____
3. outstanding _____
4. lack _____
5. fee _____
6. malign _____
7. magnify _____
8. sloppy _____
9. reinforce _____
10. ingratitude _____
11. minimize _____

A. exceptional, noticeable

B. price or charge for a service

C. speak badly of, to falsely represent as evil

D. not neat

E. strengthen, increase in power

F. interfering

G. make larger, increase in importance

H. lack of thanks, no appreciation

I. to not possess a thing or quality

J. an over-simplified opinion held by a large group of people

K. make smaller or less important

II Using Idioms

Can you use these idioms in the proper sentence?

show up   in the wrong   get rid of

a good catch   strike back

1. Janet is marrying a rich and handsome lawyer. He sure is a _____.

2. Mrs. Jones wanted some medicine to _____ the pain in her back.

3. How many people do you think will _____ at the party?

4. Mother could not decide which of the children were _____ so she punished both of them.

5. If you hit Charlie, he will probably _____.

III Discussion

1. Can you think of some of the stereotypes held about people in your country:

    a. The people in the North of my country are _____ _____.

    b. The people in the country bordering my country are _____.

    c. People who live in the capitol are _____.

    d. Country people are_____.

    e. Doctors are _____.

2. Before you came to America, what were the stereotypes you heard or held about Americans?

    Americans are _____ _____.

3. Now that you are in America, do you still think so? _____

4. What are your present feelings about Americans? _____

5. Is there a negative stereotype of mothers-in-law in your country?_____

6. Are there many jokes about mothers-in-law? _____ Sons-in-law? _____

CHAPTER FIVE: The Battle of the Sexes

Jokes about Men, Women, and Marriage

It's easy to get married. In most states, a $10 license fee, a blood test, and a three-day waiting period are the only hurdles* to cross before a couple can "tie the knot"*.

It's difficult, and expensive, to get divorced. Lawyers' fees are very high, and a divorce case takes months at the least. Some divorces cost many thousands of dollars in lawyers' fees, and the court battle may last for years. A divorce usually represents a lot of human unhappiness.

Statistics tell us that 50% of all marriages begun in the United States today will probably end in divorce. Some people have suggested that laws should change to make it as difficult and expensive to get married as it is to get divorced.

Nevertheless, most people get married, and most of the ones who later get divorced find another partner and marry again within five years.

The tensions that come with marriage, or fear of marriage and fear of divorce make these the subject of many jokes. One stereotyped idea has been that marriage is the natural state for women, and being single is the natural state for men.

<> The early part of my marriage was wonderful. The trouble began as we were leaving the church.

<> A Hollywood couple got divorced. Then they got remarried. The divorce didn't work out.

(Hollywood is the home of the movie stars, who are notorious* for marrying many times [another stereotype]).

31

<> **Bigamy*** is having one **spouse*** too many.
Monogamy* is often the same thing.

(In other words, one wife is too many.)

<> People don't know what true happiness is
until they get married. Then it's too late.

<> There are two periods in a man's life when
he doesn't understand women: before marriage and
after.

<> Jack called his friend. He was very
depressed*.
"The woman I love has just **turned me down***,"
he **moaned***. "She won't marry me."
"Don't feel so bad," his friend said, trying to
cheer him up. "A woman often says no when she
means yes."
"But she didn't say no. She said **phooey***!"

<> "For twenty years, my wife and I were very
happy."
"What happened then?"
"We met."

(We were happy before we met each other, but not after.)

<> "My wife and I had a wonderful time at the
beach. First she buried me in the sand, and then I
buried her. Next summer I'm going back and dig her
up."

<> A little old lady goes into court to ask the
judge for a divorce from her husband. The judge is
surprised. "How old are you?" he asks.
"Sixty-five years old."
"And how long have you been married?" asks
the judge.
"Forty-five years."
"Why is it you want a divorce after so many
years?"
"Ahhh, enough is enough," she says.

Women and wives

The **Women's Liberation Movement*** has caused a revolution in the way Americans think about women and wives.

There are traditional stereotypes of women, both positive and negative. These are still accepted by many people. But **feminists***, both men and women, are **struggling*** to **shatter*** the traditional stereotypes. They have been successful in getting the **media*** (TV, movies, newspapers, textbooks, etc.) to change the way they present women, men and their relationships.

(Remember, a stereotype represents lazy thinking and is often false. Traditional stereotypes of women are:

Women are gentle, soft, lovely, patient. They are good at such things as delicate hand work (typing, sewing, knitting), decorating and managing a home, cooking, listening, mothering, nursing, teaching children. Women are **passive***, weak, timid, less intelligent than men, and emotionally **unstable***. A woman needs a man to protect her, to make decisions for her and to make her life meaningful. Women are **vain*** and spend a lot of time trying to become beautiful. It takes them a long time to get dressed; they are often late for appointments.

More stereotyped attitudes: Women use tricks to trap a man into marriage. They are interested in love, but not in sex. Women are interested in men for their money rather than for their character. Women cannot understand **complex*** things such as the business world, higher mathematics and physics, or the rules of football. A wife **has it easy***, she stays at home with little to do except watch the afternoon **soap operas***. Women love to go shopping for clothes and spend more money than they (or their husbands) earn. Women talk too much. A new wife is a terrible cook.

The following jokes rely on the traditional stereotypes of women:

<> A woman told her husband that her new dress didn't cost her anything. "How's that?" he asked.
"Well, it was originally $80, but it was reduced to $40, so I bought it with the $40 I saved."

<> My wife went to a beauty parlor and got a **mud pack*** treatment. She looked really good for two days. Then the mud fell off.

<> I don't want to **criticize*** my wife's cooking, but last night she burned the potato salad.

<> A man comes home from work to find his wife crying. "What's wrong?" he asks.
"I baked you an apple pie, and the dog has just eaten it!"
"Don't worry. I'll get you another dog," he says.

(The wife is sad that her pie is gone, but the husband thinks she is crying because the dog may die from a stomach ache from eating her cooking.)

<> Mr. Jackson decided to take his wife to play golf. At the first **tee***, Jackson swung and hit the ball so hard, it went sailing over a hill. After a few minutes a very angry man came running toward the Jacksons.
"Your ball hit my wife in the head and **knocked her out*!**" yelled the other man.
"Oh, I'm really sorry," said Mr. Jackson. He gave the man his golf club. "Here, take a shot at mine."

(To show you that I am sorry for the accident, you may hit <u>my</u> wife with the ball.)

<> A man was at a bar, slowly sipping his beer and looking very gloomy.
"What's the problem?" asked the bartender. "You look so sad."
"My wife and I had a fight. She told me she wasn't going to talk to me for 30 days."
"That should make you happy!" said the bartender.
"It did," said the man. "But that was 29 days ago. Today is the last day."

<> "I have a problem," said Jack. "Every time I go to the movies, a fat lady sits next to me and **munches*** popcorn through the whole show."

"Why don't you change seats?" asked his friend Joe.

"I can't. She's my wife."

<> My wife looks really awful in the mornings. Her hair is up in curlers, her face is greasy with cold cream, there are big bags under her eyes, and her old housecoat is full of holes. The other day she ran after the garbage truck because she had forgotten to take out the trash the night before. "Am I too late for the garbage?" she says.

"No," says the driver. "Just jump right in."

It requires great effort to change stereotyped thinking. The Women's Liberation Movement has slowly made both men and women aware of the harm that the traditional stereotypes did to both sexes. Change is not easy, but there are now new images of women in jokes, stories, movies, and TV. Jokes with the traditional negative stereotypes of women are still being told by men. But fewer and fewer people think they are funny.

Men and Husbands

Stereotypes about men are changing too, thanks to the Women's Liberation Movement and the Men's Liberation Movement.

(Remember: a stereotype represents lazy thinking and is quite often false.)

Here are some traditional stereotyped attitudes about men:

Men are strong, intelligent, courageous, emotionally stable. A "real" man doesn't cry. They are good at business, math and physics, and leadership. Men are problem solvers, and the protectors of women and children. Men are unemotional, and lack sensitivity. Men are always interested in sex. Men are unromantic*, and after they feel a woman is "caught" they take her for granted*. After marriage, husbands do not pay attention to their wives. They read the newspaper through breakfast and spend their evenings in front of the TV watching a baseball game with a six-pack of beer. They cannot understand fashion, or even choose two socks that match. They are stingy with money. They are lazy and useless around the house, and clumsy* at home repairs.

<> The marriage counselor* was asking the wife about her moods*. "Do you wake up grumpy* in the morning?"
"No," she answered, "I let him sleep until breakfast is ready."

(Here there is a play on the word "grumpy." The counselor is asking the wife if she wakes up grumpy [adjective describing the wife's possible mood]. The wife interprets* the question as, "Do you wake up Grumpy?" [noun, a nick-name* for her husband, indicating HIS personality].)

<> Mrs. Lipschitz, a very wealthy woman, was wearing a huge diamond at a very fancy party. Several women gathered around to admire the diamond. "There are three famous diamonds in the world," she explained. "The Hope Diamond, the Kohiron Diamond and the Lipschitz Diamond. But the Lipschitz Diamond is the only one with a **curse.***"

"Really? asked one of the women. "What is the curse?"

"Lipschitz."

(<u>Mr</u>. Lipschitz is the world's worst husband. In order to own such a beautiful diamond, she has to live with Mr. Lipschitz.)

<> Doctor: I'm a little worried about your husband, Mrs. Wilson. I don't like the way he looks.

Mrs. Wilson: I don't either, but he's good to the children.

("I don't like the way he looks," is ambiguous: 1. He appears sick, and I am concerned about it. [the doctor's intended meaning] 2. He's not handsome or good-looking. [the wife's meaning]).

Exercises

I Vocabulary

Choose one of the words in the list that is the synonym for the word in parentheses:

shatter   passive   vain

complex   mood   munch

1. The ball hit the mirror, but luckily the glass did not _____ (break into many pieces.

2. Pat is a very _____ (shy and unaggressive) person.

3. I like to _____ (chew) on an apple after lunch.

4. The laws regarding divorce are very _____ (complicated).

5. Paul is in a bad _____ (state of mind) this morning.

6. Dan is quite _____ (conceited, self-centered) and is always looking in the mirror.

II Match the word with the definition:

1. bigamy _____   A. husband or wife

2. monogamy _____   B. a social and political
                             movement to change society's
                             attitudes and increase
                             opportunities for women

3. spouse _____   C. radio, TV, magazines, books

4. nick-name_____   D. chew noisily

5. Women's Liberation _____
                         E. bad-tempered, easily angry
6. media _____
                         F. afternoon TV drama
7. soap opera _____

8. criticize ____

9. tee ____

10. munch ____

11. grumpy ____

12. clumsy ____

13. curse ____

G. having one husband or wife

H. having two spouses

I. a golf ball is placed on this

J. a short or familiar form of a name; a name showing a quality of a person

K. to find fault with, correct

L. a very sad event or story

M. an evil wish or punishment

N. awkward, not graceful

III Discussion

1. What are the traditional stereotypes of men in your country?

2. What are the stereotypes of women?

3. Do women in your country have careers after they are married?

4. Has the Women's Liberation Movement had any effect in your country?

5. How are marriages arranged in your country?

6. How common is divorce?

7. Are there great social penalties for divorce in your country?

8. Tell the class a joke about marriage or divorce in your country.

CHAPTER SIX: Parents and Children (and Dogs)

Some parents think their own children are perfect. They brag* about them, show their pictures, and tell anecdotes* about their cuteness until everyone is bored by them. Other people think the children are rude, thoughtless, noisy, and destructive.

<> There is only one beautiful child in the world . . . and every parent has it.

<>Earthquake* tremors* were being felt all over San Francisco. A couple sent their small son to visit with his aunt and uncle who lived in a safer area. After a few days, they got a telegram: "We are sending back little Timmy. Please send earthquake instead."

<> "I thought you and your wife were going to get a divorce.
"It fell through*. Neither of us wanted custody* of the children."

The Jewish Mother

This caricature* of All Mothers is responsible for a great deal of gentle fun. In the stereotype, the Jewish Mother over-protects her children, sacrifices* for them, and makes them feel guilty about their actions. She is impossible to please. Whenever anyone is sick, she prepares chicken soup for them. (Chicken soup is sometimes known as Jewish penicillin.) She pushes her children to become (or marry) doctors, dentists, or lawyers, and brags with great pride when they are successful.

<> A Jewish Mother gave her son two shirts for his birthday. To show her how much he appreciated the gift, he went to his room and immediately put on

40

one of the shirts.

His mother looked at him and said, "So, what's the matter, didn't you like the other one?"

<> Did you hear about the Jewish Mother who had two pet chickens? One of them got sick, so she killed the other one to make soup for it.

Dog Owners

Dog owners are like parents, in a way, always bragging about their own dogs. Their bragging is exaggerated in many dog jokes.

<> Several men were sitting around bragging about how smart their dogs are.

"My dog is so smart," said the first one, "that I can send him out to the store for eggs. He sniffs around the boxes and refuses to accept any boxes unless they are fresh."

"My dog is so smart," said the second man, "that he goes out for cigars, and he always comes home with my favorite brand. "

The two men turned to a third man who had been sitting quietly. "Have you ever heard of any dog that is as smart as ours?" asked the first man.

"Well, only one dog. Mine."

"How is that?"

"My dog **runs*** the store where your dogs go shopping."

<> He: My dog is lost.

She: Why don't you put an ad in the paper?

He: Silly, that won't do any good. My dog can't read!

42

Exercises

I Vocabulary

Choose the correct word for each sentence:

brag   anecdotes   custody   caricature

1. An artist drew a _____ of Jack, exaggerating his features.

2. Mr. Jackson likes to tell _____ about his boyhood days on the farm.

3. It isn't polite to _____ about your own achievements.

4. At the divorce trial, the judge gave _____ of the children to their mother.

Discussion

1. Is it considered polite in your country to brag about your own children?

2. Are parents stricter with their children in your country than in America? Are children better behaved here or in your country?

3. Do many people have dogs as pets in your country? What is the attitude towards pets?

CHAPTER SEVEN: College Life

life.   There are many stereotypes of college students and college

College life brings intellectual **challenges***, social opportunities and many tensions.   Students have to **adjust*** to life in a **dormitory***, and share **quarters*** with a roommate. Grades must be kept up; there is the daily **grind*** of attending classes that are not always interesting, researching   endless **term papers,*** and **cramming*** for exams.   These are all **anxiety-provoking*** experiences.

Some students take college very seriously, while others are there to have a good time.   One stereotype is that college is seen by women as a place to find a husband.   (This is referred to as getting an M.R.S. degree.   i.e., marrying a male student and becoming <u>Mrs</u>. **So and So*.**)

There are stereotypes of professors who demand perfection from their students, or who are unfair, **pompous***, **absent-minded*** or boring. Other stereotypes are of "know-it-all" students who study hard, do well on tests, **butter up*** the professors, and get all A's.   The stereotyped lazy student sleeps in class, cheats on tests, and avoids difficult courses.

Colleges have a sports program   and   winning football or basketball teams can be a financial help to a college.   For this reason, there are scholarships to attract good athletes to a college.   In the stereotype, these athletes are poor students, but they must have passing grades to stay on the team.

There are many complaints about college food.   Cafeteria food is never like "Mom's home cooking."   The stereotype is that it is overcooked, underflavored, and sometimes unrecognizable.

All night parties and drinking are common in the stereotype of behavior on **campus***.   Many jokes involve an acceptance of drunkenness, and an exaggeration of the wildness of parties.

44

Parents may still have to **foot the bills***, but would probably disapprove of some of the new behavior their grown children are adopting.

<> Three college seniors were wondering what to do on a Sunday evening. "I've got an idea, said one. Let's **toss a coin***. If it's **heads***, we'll go to the sophomore dance and look for girls; if it's **tails*** we'll go out drinking. And if it stands on edge . . . we'll study!"

<> (In the college cafeteria)
Assistant manager: The garbage trucks are here.
Manager: OK. Tell them to leave three cans.

(Garbage trucks generally <u>take away</u> garbage. They <u>bring</u> garbage <u>to</u> this cafeteria. That's why the food is so bad.)

<> Mack, to his roommate: Hey, Joe, that's <u>my</u> raincoat you're wearing.
Joe: Well, you wouldn't want your new suit to get wet, would you?

(The roommate has borrowed clothes without permission.)

<> A father was driving home from an out-of-town business appointment. He had to pass through his son's college town late at night. He decided to pay a surprise visit to his son even though it was quite late. He came to the **fraternity house*** and knocked on the door but no one came to open it. He continued to knock until finally someone opened the second floor window.
"Whadda ya want?"
"Does Jim Jackson live here?"
"Yeah, just carry him in."

(The person at the window is apparently accustomed to Jim Jackson's getting so drunk he cannot walk. He does not know that the man is Jackson's father. He thinks that it is someone who has helped to bring Jackson home.)

45

<> A star football player **flunked*** his math course. The coach was very upset and went to the professor to beg him to give the boy another chance. Finally the professor agreed to a special exam.

When it was over and the professor had corrected the test, the coach asked, "Well, how did he do?"

"He flunked again. It looks hopeless." The professor showed the coach the paper. "Look at this--6 x 7 = 45."

"Oh, **gee whiz***, prof," said the coach. "**Give him a break***. He only missed it by one."

(i.e., the coach thinks 6 x 7 = 44 and so is not any smarter than the player.)

<> Written on textbook covers:

The more we study, the more we know.
The more we know, the more we forget.
The more we forget, the less we know.
The less we know, the less we forget.
The less we forget, the more we know.
So why study?

<> "If the **dean*** doesn't **take back*** what he said to me this morning, I'm going to leave college," said the student.

"What did he say?" asked his roommate.

"He told me to leave college."

<> Professor: You can't sleep in my class!
Student: I could if you didn't talk so loud.

<> Student # 1: The Dean announced that he's going to stop drinking on campus.
Student # 2: No kidding! Next thing you know, he'll want us to stop drinking, too.

("Stop drinking on campus" is an ambiguous sentence. The first student's meaning is: The dean is going to stop <u>the</u>

students' drinking.   The second student interprets it as, the
dean is going to stop [his own] drinking on campus.

      <> Father: What was the hardest thing you
learned at college?
          Son: How to open beer bottles with a
half-dollar.

      <> "I hear that the water you get at the
dormitory is unsafe to drink.   What do you do about
it?"
      "Well, first we boil it."
      "Yes."
      "Then we **filter*** it."
      "Yes."
      "Then we add chemicals to kill any remaining
bacteria*."
      "Yes."
      "Then we drink beer."

Exercises

I Vocabulary

Choose a word from the list to complete the following sentences:

term paper	quarters	pompous	take back
flunk	grind	butter up	
ambitious	campus	foot the bills	
toss a coin			

1. If you _____ your boss before you ask
him for a raise, you may be more successful.

2. Dan was upset because he thought he would _____
his chemistry exam.

3. Mrs. Jackson was bored with the daily _____ of
cleaning house, shopping, cooking, doing laundry, and paying

bills.

4. Jack doesn't have much money. Who will ____ ____
_____ if he goes to medical school?

5. Barbara spent six hours in the library doing research for her
_____.

6. If you can't decide whether to go to the movies or go ice
skating, why don't you _____?

7. Dick and his girlfriend had a big fight. He said a lot of
angry things to her and now wishes he could _____ his
words.

8. I visited Carl in his new dormitory. His living
_____ are small, but very pleasant and neat.

9. Professor Holmes has a very _____
attitude. He acts as if he owned the university..

10. Paul is very _____. He wants to be a
millionaire by the age of thirty.

11. The University of Maine certainly has a beautiful
_____. It's surrounded by woods and lakes.

II Discussion

1. What is the stereotype of a college student in your country?

2. How is a college professor stereotyped in your country?

3. Do you think college students are more serious about studies
in your country?

4. What jokes about students, studies, or professors can you tell
the class?

CHAPTER EIGHT: The People in Power

Policemen, politicians, bosses, teachers, landlords, and religious leaders are the voices of authority. They make the rules and have the power to **enforce*** them. If we don't follow the rules, we can be arrested, fired from our jobs, failed in school, **evicted*** from our homes, or kept out of Heaven.

So most of the time, most of us follow most of the rules. The resentment is expressed in humor, and we can strike back at those in authority without **risking*** our freedom or safety.

Boss jokes illustrate the negative stereotype of bosses: They are demanding, stingy, and always fooling around with their attractive secretaries. The boss hires his own son at a high salary, but the son is thoroughly **incompetent***. No one, however, can say a word against the young man.

<> A boss was known for his strict demand that his employees be **punctual***. One day one of the workers showed up an hour late. He was walking on **crutches***, and had **bruises*** all over his face. The boss looked at the clock and looked at the employee. "Why are you late?"
"I fell down the stairs," said the **timid*** employee.
"And that took you an hour?" the boss shouted.

<> It was the first day of school, and Mrs. Stein found her son crying in the kitchen.
"You'd better hurry, you'll be late for school."
"I don't want to go!"
"What's the matter?"
"I don't have any friends there, and the teachers all hate me!"
"Well, you'll just have to go anyway. After all, you <u>are</u> the principal."

(We are surprised because we thought Mrs. Stein was talking to a <u>little boy</u>. When we find out her son is the principal, we see different reasons for him to have no friends and for all the teachers to hate him.)

The landlord is usually stereotyped in humor as **greedy***. He supplies few services, and asks for more rent than the house is worth. Before a tenant moves in, the landlord tells lies about the advantages of the apartment, and hides the disadvantages.

<> New tenant: Does the water always come through the roof like this?
Landlord: No. Only when it rains.

<> A tourist was visiting a castle.
"This castle has stood for 600 years. Nothing has been touched in that time, not a stone has been changed, nothing replaced," said the guide.
"Hmm," said the tourist. "They must have the same landlord I have."

The President, senators, congressmen, and other leaders of the country are the constant butts of humor. Many joke writers read each day's newpapers carefully to find out what ways the government is **irritating*** the people. These irritations are the basis for the jokes told on the evening television talk shows.

Americans **prize*** the freedom to **poke fun at*** our leaders. This is often surprising to visitors and immigrants from other countries. There are many countries where this is not allowed, or where there is great respect for the position of the leaders. We find it a great **safety valve*** in the complex relations between government and the people.

Of course Democrats will poke fun at the Republicans and the Republicans will poke fun at the Democrats. Both will poke fun at Communists, Socialists, and other political groups. The **party in power*** is seen as being responsible for the various problems of taxation, unemployment, **inflation***, **scandal***, and mismanagement.

<> President Reagan was discussing the economy with a **stockbroker***. The stockbroker was

51

arguing about how poor **the economy*** was looking.
"The economy is looking much better," said the
President. "As a matter of fact, if I weren't
president, I would buy some **stocks*** right now."
(There is a law against the president owning any
business or stocks.)
"If you weren't president," said the
stockbroker, "I'd buy stocks, too."

(The stockbroker means that if Reagan weren't President,
the economy of the country would be much better and it would be
safe to buy stocks.)

The stereotype of politicians is not very **flattering***: They
make promises to get elected and break the promises as soon as
they are in office. They waste the taxpayers' money. They are
insincere, **long-winded***, and dishonest. They do political favors
for their own families, friends, and large contributors to their
campaign funds.

<> The congressman decided to visit an Indian
tribe in his district. He prepared a long speech.
When he got to the meeting place, many Indians were
there waiting to listen to his speech. But the
congressman was disappointed to learn that only one
of the Indians could speak English.
"Don't worry," said the Indian. You make your
speech and I will translate it for you into our
language."
So the congressman spoke, and paused at the
end of each paragraph while the Indian translated.
After the translation, the rest of the Indians all
cried, **"Umgawa***, umgawa!"
"What does that mean?" asked the congressman.
"It means they like your speech," said the
translator.
The congressman felt very good about that and
continued talking a long time. After each translation
he heard the Indians cry "Umgawa." He was very
pleased with himself.
After the speech, the Indian chief invited the
congressman to take a tour around the Indian's land.
First they had to go through a cow **pasture***. As
they were walking, the chief spoke to the
congressman in Indian language, and kept pointing to
the ground. The congressman did not understand
him.
"What did he say?" he asked the translator.

"Oh, the chief wants you to be careful. He says be careful. Don't step in the umgawa."

(Umgawa is a word invented just for this joke: a vulgar Indian word for cow **manure***. The Indians had not really liked the speech at all, but had been angry, calling his promises "cow manure." The translator had been too polite to tell the truth.)

<> A Republican **candidate*** was trying to get votes by speaking to people on the street.
"No, I won't vote for you," said one man. "My father was a Democrat, and before him my grandfather was a Democrat, so I won't vote any way but Democrat."
"That's not reasonable," said the Republican candidate. "If your father had been a horse thief, and your grandfather before him had been a horse thief, would that make you a horse thief?"
"No, I guess in that case, I'd be a Republican."

(The candidate has tried to show the voter than he is not logical in remaining a Democrat just because his father and grandfather were Democrats. The voter happily twists the intentions of the candidate and implies that horse thieves and Republicans come from the same families.

<> A farmer had seventeen children. When they grew up, they all voted Democratic, all except one boy, who voted Republican.
"How do you explain that your boys all vote Democratic except for John?" asked a friend.
"Well, I've always tried to raise my boys right, work hard, go to church, and become Democrats just like their Pa. But John, there, was an **ornery*** one and learned how to read."

(By reading, he became educated, and made a smarter choice.)

<> A little boy's cat had had kittens and the boy was trying to find homes for them. The Democrats

were having a big political **convention*** in his town, near his house, so he sat near the convention door and asked each person if they would like a kitten.

"Are these Democratic kittens?" asked a man attending the convention.

"Oh, yes, sir."

"Then I'll take two."

A few weeks later, the boy still had not found homes for the remaining three kittens. The Republican Convention came, and he again went near the convention hall.

"What kind of kittens are they?" asked a lady.

"Why, they're Republican kittens," the boy answered.

A hot dog vendor on the street interrupted him. "Now, listen here," he said. "Two weeks ago you were here and you told a Democrat that these were Democratic kittens. Now you're telling this lady that they are Republican kittens. How do you explain that?"

"Well, now these kittens have their eyes open," said the boy.

(i.e., they are smarter now, so they have changed political parties.)

National, state and local governments have many confusing laws and regulations that complicate the lives of the people. **Bureaucrats*** are the people who work for the government. They are stereotyped in jokes as lazy, unhelpful, and irritating. Government projects are very slow. Anyone dealing with the government is sure to be confused and frustrated by **red tape.***

<> "I hear your husband tried to get a government job. What is he doing now?"
"Nothing."
"Oh. Didn't he get the job?"
"Yes, he did."

<> The tourist was seeing the **Grand Canyon*** for first time.
"Do you realize," said the guide, "that it took millions and millions of years for this great canyon to be formed?"
"Oh, really?" said the tourist. "I didn't know it was a government job."

<> A politician's son needed a job, so the politician spoke to the head of a government department. "My boy would like to work in your department," he said.
"What can he do?" asked the department head.
"Nothing."
"That makes it simple. We won't have to waste time training him for the job."

<> A politician who was running for office became very angry at the editor of a newspaper. "You are telling lies about me in your paper, and you know it!"
"That's nothing to complain about," said the editor. "You should really worry what would happen if we told the truth about you."

We have police for our protection and safety. While we need, and sometimes appreciate, our police forces, there are some negative stereotypes.

<> A policeman called **headquarters*** on the car radio. "A man has been robbed down here, and I've got one of them."

"Which one do you have?" asked the chief

"The one who was robbed."

(The police could only catch the innocent victim, not the robber.)

<> A cop was directing traffic on Fifth Avenue one day and everything was going along very nicely. Suddenly people started running, screaming, and climbing up trees; cars and taxis started to honk their horns, and drive into each other and up on to the sidewalks. Pretty soon the cop saw what was causing the problem. Walking down the street was a man with an enormous alligator on a **leash***.

The cop, very brave, goes near the man and points his finger at the alligator. "Take that alligator to the Central Park Zoo!" he yells.

"That's a good idea," says the man, and he walks off towards the zoo.

The next day the same cop is directing traffic on the same corner on Fifth Avenue. Everything is peaceful until suddenly people start to run and scream and climb up the trees, and cars and buses are crashing into each other. What could it be this time, wonders the cop.

Along comes the same man, with the same alligator on a leash, walking down the street.

"Hey, Mister, I thought I told you to take that alligator to the Central Park Zoo!"

"I did," said the man. "And he liked it so much that today we're going to the Museum of Natural History!"

Religion supplies us with answers to the Unknowable. Our religious leaders are supposed to be free of the faults that the rest of us have. God is **Omnipotent***, and Heaven is a Perfect Place. Jokes about religion show that there is also room for doubt.

<> A Jew says to his friend: "Do you know

that my **rabbi*** talks with God every day?
"How do you know that?"
"He told me."
"But suppose he is lying?"
"Don't be a fool. How could a rabbi who
speaks with God every day dare to tell a lie?"

(Here there is totally illogical thinking on the
part of the first person.)

Saint Peter*, in popular Christian folklore is the person in
charge of tending the Gates to Heaven. (The Pearly Gates)
Many jokes use this character and this setting.

<> A man died and went to heaven. He met
Saint Peter at the Gate and St. Peter took him to the
supply house. "Here are your wings," he said, and
handed the man a pair of rather worn-out looking
wings. "And here is your **harp***," he said, and
handed him a **tarnished*** harp with several strings
missing. The man played the harp for a minute and
found that it was **out of tune***. "And here is your
own private cloud. It will take you anywhere in
Heaven that you want to go." The cloud was gray
and all covered with dirt.
The man looked at his new things and said to
St. Peter, "I thought this was Heaven, and
everything was supposed to be beautiful. But you
give me worn-out wings, a harp that is out of tune,
and a dirty gray cloud."
"I'm sorry," said St. Peter, "that's the best
we can do. Everyone has the same thing."
"Well, if it's the best you can do, I guess I'll
have to be satisfied," said the man, and he put on
his wings and got on his cloud and went slowly
floating around playing his awful-sounding harp. He
saw a lot of people, and it was true, they all had the
same as he had, so he stopped feeling so bad. Then
all of a sudden, a fellow on a beautiful shiny white
jet-propelled cloud came **whooshing*** by. He had a
pair of beautiful wings and was playing music on the
loveliest sounding harp you could imagine.
The man went right back to St. Peter and
asked him, "Hey, I thought everyone in Heaven was
supposed to be equal. How come that one guy has a
snow-white, jet-propelled cloud, beautiful wings, and
a terrific sounding harp?"

"Shhhh," said St. Peter. "It's the Boss's son."

(The Boss = God. The man on the beautiful cloud is Jesus. In Heaven, just as in a business, the son of the boss has all the advantages.)

<> One Sunday a **nun*** and a priest were playing golf. The priest was having a hard time hitting the ball in the right direction. First he swung the club and the ball went flying right into a lake. "Darn it, missed," he said, and swore out loud using very **obscene*** language. The next time he swung, he sent the ball into a sand trap. "Darn it, missed again!" and he added other obscene words in his anger.

"You shouldn't be swearing and using obscene language on the **Sabbath***," said the nun.

But the priest continued playing badly and when he hit a ball that flew into the woods, he said, "Darn it, missed again!" and swore even worse.

"That's terrible!" said the nun. I hope God strikes you dead with a **bolt of lightning*** if you use that bad language one more time!

The priest ignored her, swung at the ball, and hit it into a tree, where it got stuck in a bird's nest. He said, "Darn it! Missed again!", and swore even worse than the other times.

All of a sudden the sky blackened. There was a terrible clap of thunder, and a huge bolt of lightning shot out of a cloud and struck . . . the nun. She fell over dead.

A deep voice came from up in the clouds. "Darn it! Missed again!"

60

(The voice was God's. The joke's message is that God is not perfect. Not only did He miss the priest whom he had intended to hit with the bolt of lightning, He swears and blasphemes the same way the priest does. The nun got killed, even though it was by accident. The butt of the joke, the nun, represents the **goodie goodies***, who are always telling other people how to behave.)

<> Two painters are high up on **scaffolds*** repairing the ceiling of the **Sistine Chapel*** at Saint Peter's Cathedral in Rome. They look down and see an old Italian woman **saying her rosary*** and praying. "Watch this," says one painter to the other. "I'm going to give her the surprise of her life." He shapes his hands over his mouth and calls out in a low voice directed at the woman, "I am the son of God." There is no reaction, the woman goes on praying.

Again, he does the same thing. "I am the son of God." Again, there's no reaction from the woman. He tries a third time, a little louder. "I am the son of God!"

At this the old woman looks up very annoyed. "Shut-uppa you face," she says. "I'm-a talk to your mother."

(Catholics may pray to God, to Jesus, or to the Virgin Mary, the Mother of Jesus, as well as to any of the Saints. Rosary beads are used to keep count of the number of prayers said. The use of an Italian accent and rude manner of speaking increase the impact of the joke. Shut up = be quiet. Shut your face. = Shut your mouth. I'm-a talk = I'm talking)

Exercises

I Vocabulary

Choose the best answer to complete the following sentences:

1. An incompetent person ____   A. is exactly on time.

2. A punctual person ____   B. is an injury where the skin is not broken.

3. A crutch____   C. is a general increase in prices.

4. A bruise ____   D. is Sunday, or a holy day of rest.

5. Inflation ____   E. is unfit for a job; unable to do things.

6. Red-tape ____   F. is a musical instrument.

7. A pasture ____   G. is a person who works for a government agency.

8. A stockbroker ____   H. difficulty and confusion caused by government regulations and official forms.

9. A bureaucrat ____   I. is an area where cows may eat grass.

10. A scandal ____   J. is improper and shameful acts or behavior that become publicly known.

11. A harp ____   K. is a person who acts as an agent in the buying and selling of stocks.

12. Sabbath ____   L. helps a person with a broken leg to walk.

II The following words all have a religious connection. Can you find the correct definition?

Saint Peter (St. Peter)   nun   priest   rabbi

Pearly Gates   Sabbath   chapel

rosary beads   services   blasphemy

1. A woman who devotes her life to the Catholic church
_____

2. A leader of a Jewish congregation _____

3. A leader of a Catholic congregation _____

4. In Christian folklore, the entrance to Heaven
_____

5. The person who tends the entrance to Heaven
_____

6. A device to help count the number of prayers said
_____

7. The religious rites or ceremonies at a church or temple
_____

8. Words or acts that dishonor God _____

9. A day of rest and religious services _____

10. A small church, or part of a church
_____

III Discussion

1. Who is the head of the government in your country? Is it common to hear jokes about this leader on TV shows? In public? In private?

2. What is the stereotype for a lawmaker in your country?

3. Are policemen respected, feared, or ridiculed in your country?

4. Is there one dominant religion in your country or several? Are jokes about religious leaders or God common?

63

5. Are there political parties in your country? Are there jokes about these parties?

6. Can you tell the class a joke about a "Person in Power" in your country?

CHAPTER NINE: Doctors, Psychiatrists, and Their Patients

Medicine is one of the most respected and well-rewarded professions in America. Doctors, however, are not perfect, and medicine is considered an "art, not a science." The doctor's "bedside manner*" is as important to the patient's recovery* as his medical skill.

In the American stereotype, the doctor charges high fees for a few minutes service, after the patient has waited hours to see him. The doctor wants to be trusted, but he does not always know the answers.

Illness and surgery* provoke* anxiety. Patients and their families worry about wrong diagnoses* and unnecessary operations. It is now common for a patient to go to another doctor to get a "second opinion" before having an operation.

Today, most doctors in the United States are specialists*. They are experts in one field of medicine, but know very little about others. People become frustrated* when they have to deal with different specialists for different parts of their bodies when they are sick.

Jokes help us deal with this anxiety by exaggerating the pains and exaggerating the inability* of doctors to deal with them.

<> A man went to the doctor with a terrible pain in his arm. The doctor examined it, and looked very puzzled.* He studied his medical books, but could not find any answers. "Have you ever had this pain before?" the doctor finally asked.
"Yes, doctor."
"Well," said the doctor, "you've got it again."

<> "Doctor, when my hands are out of the casts*, will I be able to play the piano?"

"Yes, Mrs. Jones."
"Oh goody. I could never play before!"

<> Doctor: Did you **consult*** anyone else before you came to see me?
Patient: Yes, I spoke to the owner of the **health food*** store.
Doctor: And what foolish thing did he tell you to do?
Patient: He told me to see you.

<> "Doctor, Doctor!" said the patient. "I have a potato growing in my ear!"
The doctor looked in the patient's ear and said, "Oh, my goodness, so you have! This is most unusual!"
"Yes!" said the patient, very **upset***. "I planted carrots!"

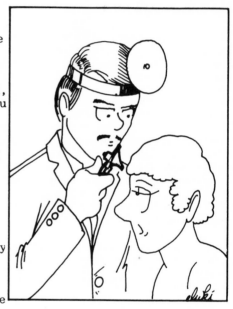

<> Our doctor would never **recommend*** surgery unless it was really necessary. If he didn't absolutely need the money, he'd never operate on you.

<> News Flash: Medical **researchers*** have just discovered a cure for which there is no known disease.

<> "Doctor I'm worried about this operation you're going to do. Dr. White operated on my friend for **lung*** disease, and he died of heart disease."

66

"Don't worry," said the doctor. "When I treat a patient for lung disease, my patient dies from lung disease."

<> A man went to a doctor and was told he had a serious illness and would need an operation.
"Is it very dangerous?"
"Yes, it is. Four out of five people who have this operation die. But you will have nothing to worry about!"
"Why not?"
"I have already operated on four people and they have all died."

Each of us has mental problems and **irrational*** thoughts at times. The only thing that separates us from people who are **insane*** is the **degree*** and frequency of those thoughts. Today, there are a very large number of professionals who are trained to help people with emotional or family problems.

In recent years, more and more Americans have been turning to psychotherapy to find ways to make better decisions, solve emotional problems, improve their health, increase their creativity and deal with life's difficulties in a more effective way. Our complex society has created many problems that never existed in a more simple environment.

However, not everyone who could use help gets it. Many people are too embarrassed to go for it. For some people, there is a social **stigma*** attached to seeing a psychiatrist. These people fear that others will think they are crazy if they go for help with their emotional problems. Others feel that it is just too expensive. Many health insurance plans now pay for treatment for mental health as well as physical health.

Psychiatrists, psychoanalysts, psychologists, and psychotherapists* are terms for different specialists. The public often confuses the terms and **lumps them all together*** under the term psychiatrist.

When we laugh at jokes about psychiatrists and their patients, or the **inmates*** of mental institutions, we **reduce*** tension about our own occasional unexplainable behavior or thoughts.

The stereotype of the psychiatrist is that he is a little **nutty*** himself.

67

<> Anyone who sees a psychiatrist ought to have his head examined.

<> **Neurotics*** are people who build castles in the air.
Psychotics* are people who live in them.
Psychiatrists are the people who collect the rent.

(To build castles in the air = have dreams or fantasies not based on reality.)

<> "Doctor, you've got to help me. I think I am **losing my mind***. I can't remember anything any more," said the new patient.
"I see," said the psychiatrist. "How long have you had this problem?"
"What problem?"

<>A psychiatrist asked his patient what he dreamed about at night.
"Baseball," said the patient.
"Don't you ever dream about other things?"
"No, just baseball every night."
The psychiatrist had difficulty believing this.
"Don't you ever dream about girls?"
"What! And miss my turn at bat?"

(In baseball, the team players take turns "at bat." The patient does not want to miss his turn. Dreaming about girls would interfere with this more important activity.) (Many girls and women find that their boyfriends and husbands often pay more attention to baseball than to them.)

<> A new patient had his first meeting with a psychiatrist. After asking many questions, and listening to the patient for a long time, the psychiatrist said, "Well, there's no doubt about it: you're crazy."

68

The patient stood up and got very angry. "Hmmph!" he said. "I'd like to get a second opinion!"

"All right then," said the psychiatrist. "You're ugly, too."

<> "I'm always forgetting things," said the patient to his new psychiatrist. "What should I do?" "Pay me in advance."

<> At a psychiatrists' convention, the young psychiatrist asked an older psychiatrist for advice. "I am always so upset and exhausted with my patients' problems. You look very **carefree*** and youthful. How do you manage it, listening year after year to your patients' fears, anxieties, and emotional problems?"

The older psychiatrist looked at the younger one. "Who listens?" he said.

<> A very disturbed-looking man went into the psychiatrist's office, sat down, ripped open a pack of cigarettes, took out a cigarette and shoved the cigarette up his nose.

The psychiatrist was shocked to see the man was so disturbed as to put a cigarette up his nose, and he ran toward the man. "I see you really need my help!"

"Yes, I sure do," said the patient. "Got **a light*?**"

<> "Doctor, my husband thinks he's a chicken," said the concerned wife to the psychiatrist.

"Well, we'll **straighten him out***," said the psychiatrist.

"That would be great, except for one thing," said the wife.

"What's that?"

"We need the eggs."

<> The psychiatrist was called to make a **house**

call*. "Doctor," said the woman. "Our son thinks he's a light bulb. He spends the whole night up on the ceiling."

The psychiatrist stood on a chair and slowly turned the boy around and around and took him down. "There, I unscrewed him."

"What should we do now?" asked the mother. "Work in the dark?"

(Everyone in the joke is crazy. Now that the boy is not a lightbulb anymore, the mother feels that it will be dark.)

<> A visitor to a mental institution spoke to one of the inmates. "Why do you say you are Napoleon Bonaparte? The last time I was here, you said you were Julius Caesar."

"Oh, that was by my first wife," explained the inmate.

(A woman takes her husband's name and social position when she is married. In jokes, crazy people often have delusions that they are some famous person. Napoleon, or God, are common examples. Here, the inmate is so crazy he has changed his identity by imagining marrying a different woman.)

Exercises

I Vocabulary

Choose words from the list that will best complete the sentences:

bedside manner   recovery   specialist

diagnosis   cast   consult

irrational   surgery   psychotherapist

1. Jane's doctor has recommended a _____ to treat her injured knee.

2. Dr. White's _____ is very pleasant. All of his patients like him very much.

3. It is difficult to make an accurate _____ in every case.

4. Jonathan has to wear a _____ on his leg for six weeks.

5. The patient made a quick _____ from his illness.

6. Most of us have occasional _____ thoughts, but we are not insane.

7. It can be helpful for some people to see a _____ when they have emotional problems that they cannot solve by themselves.

8. My doctor says I need _____ to remove my appendix.

9. I am going to _____ another doctor to get a second opinion.

II Discussion

1. Are doctors highly respected in your country?

2. Is there a shortage of doctors? Is there a long wait to see the doctor?

3. Is there socialized medicine, or do people have to pay for medical services?

4. What are some stereotyped ideas of doctors in your country?

5. Is it common for people to seek counseling for emotional or family problems in your country?

6. What is the stereotype of a psychiatrist in your country?

7. Can you tell the class some jokes about doctors, psychiatrists, or their patients?

CHAPTER TEN: Lawyers, Waiters, and Barbers

Law is one of the best-paid professions in the country today, and lawyers are generally highly respected in their communities.

But in American humor, the stereotyped lawyer is a liar. Lawyers' fees are too high; they talk in "double talk"*. A smart lawyer can prove that black is white. A crook* with a good lawyer can avoid going to jail. Lawyers encourage divorce battles. They follow ambulances* to talk to injured people to convince then to sue* the person who injured them. (The lawyer gets 1/3 to 1/2 of the amount sued for.)

<> "Do you have a criminal* lawyer in this town?"
"Yes we do, but we haven't been able to prove anything yet."

(A criminal lawyer is one who defends criminals. The person answering the question implies that the lawyer is a criminal.)

<> Two lawyers were talking about business.
"How are you making out?" asked the first.
"Lousy*. Business is so bad, I followed an ambulance for twelve miles and when it got to the hospital I found a lawyer already in it."

<> The friend of the judge dropped in one morning to watch the operations of the court. "You have a lot of tough-looking criminals to try* this morning, don't you? If you ask me, they all look guilty."
"Not quite," said the judge. "You are looking at the wrong bunch of people. Those are the lawyers."

74

There are many inexpensive restaurants in America, and many of them are quite good. Others are referred to as "**greasy spoons***." In the stereotype of these cheaper restaurants, the food is terrible, the kitchen is dirty, and the service is poor. The waiters in jokes are stereotyped as slow and rude. They will say there is nothing wrong with the food when the customer complains about it. They expect **generous*** tips for very poor service.

<> "Waiter, I ordered your special creamed **lobster***, and I can't find any cream and I don't see any lobster."
"Yes, sir. That's what makes it so special."

<> "Look here, waiter. If this is coffee, I want tea; but if this is tea, then I want coffee."

<> Diner: Waiter, I can't eat this food. Please call the manager.
Waiter: It's no use, sir, he won't eat it either.

<> A poor, hungry man walked into a diner and gave his order to the waitress. "I would like some **stew***, please--and a few kind words."
In a few minutes, the waitress was back with the bowl of stew. "Here you are sir."
"And what about my few kind words?"
She whispered in his ear, "Don't eat the stew!"

<> "Waiter, is this apple pie or peach pie? It tastes like glue!"
"Well then, sir, it's peach pie. Our apple pie tastes like cardboard."

A famous first line of a joke about restaurant food is this:
"Waiter, there's a fly in my soup!"   There are many different
answers to the question:

<> "Waiter, there's a fly in my soup!"
"Hush sir, all the other customers will want
one, too."

(The waiter is implying that the fly is a good thing to have
in the soup, and they may not have enough to give to everyone
if the other customers ask for flies too.)

<> "Waiter, there 's a fly in my soup!"
"Well, what do you want for 75 cents, a
mouse?"

(Seventy five cents is very cheap for a bowl of soup, so
the customer should be satisfied with a fly. A mouse in the soup
would cost much more.)

76

<> "Waiter, there's a fly in my soup."
"Yes, we ran out of bees."

(We usually have bees in the soup, but there are no more,
so we substituted flies.)

<> "Waiter, there's a fly in my soup!"
"All right, I'll bring you a fork."

<> "Waiter, there's a fly in my soup!"
"That's all right, he won't drink much."

<> "Waiter, there's a fly in my soup!"
"That's OK, there's a spider on your bread."

Waiters can strike back, too. Some customers are rude and
hard to please. They are the butts of these jokes:

<> "Waiter, do you serve crabs here?" asks a
customer.
"We serve everybody. Just have a seat at this
table, sir."

(This joke relies on the double meaning of the word crab,
as well as the double uses of the verb serve. The question the
customer asks is ambiguous. The customer meant, 1. Do you
serve crabs [a shellfish] [to people]?
The waiter insults the customer by misinterpreting the
question, since the words can also mean, 2. Do you serve
[food] to crabs [irritable and complaining people]?)

<> A customer in a restaurant was loud, rude
and disturbing to the other customers.
"What do I have to do to get a glass of water
in this **dump***?"

"Why don't you set yourself on fire?" asked an annoyed customer at the next table.

(If he sets himself on fire, someone will surely bring water to put the fire out and he can have a glass of water.)

<> Customer: This soup isn't fit* for a pig!
Waiter: I'll see if we have any that is, sir.

(The customer means that the food is terrible, and not good enough for a pig. The waiter is implying* that the customer is a pig.)

A skilled barber rarely cuts a customer while shaving him. But the razor is sharp, and an occasional accident can happen. The stereotyped barber talks constantly, and frequently slips with the razor.

<> Barber: Sir, would you mind turning the other side of your face toward me?
Customer: Are you through shaving this side?
Barber: No, but I can't stand the sight of blood.

<> The customer noticed that the barber's dog was sitting very near the barber's chair and watching him get his hair cut. "Your dog likes to watch you cut hair, doesn't he?" said the customer.
"Well, it isn't that. Sometimes I cut off a bit of ear."

<> A man went into a barber shop, sat down in the barber's chair and asked for a shave. There was a new young barber's assistant there for the first time. He spoke to the older barber: "Boss, may I try shaving this customer?"
"All right," said the boss. "Go ahead. But be careful. Don't cut yourself."
(The assistant is so inexperienced that the barber is worried that he might cut himself. If he's that bad, he will surely cut the customer, but that doesn't concern the barber.

79

Exercises

I Vocabulary

Match with word with the best definition:
1. double-talk____   A. a shellfish

2. lobster____   B. a van to transport sick people

3. criminal____   C. giving freely

4. generous ____   D. a thick soup

5. stew____   E. give a certain meaning to a
                            statement

6. imply____   F. complex speech using little-known
                            words

7. fit____   G. a robber, murderer, mugger,
                            thief, etc.

8. ambulance____   H. suitable for, appropriate for

II Discussion

1. What is the stereotype of a lawyer in your country?

2. What is the stereotype of a barber?

3. Do people make fun of waiters and restaurant food in your country?

4. Can you tell the class a joke about a lawyer, a waiter, or a barber?

CHAPTER ELEVEN: Nobody is Perfect

Most of us have secret worries about our looks, our brains, our social status and our abilities. These worries are **magnified*** when we compare ourselves with beautiful movie or TV stars, or the famous people who make the news. Our heroes seem perfect, while we are too fat or too thin, bald, forgetful, old, or unattractive. Exaggerating our own or others' **shortcomings*** in jokes makes us feel smarter, better-looking, and superior.

Some people may poke fun at their own defects or imperfections. A fat person might tell jokes about fat people, or a bald person may tell jokes about bald people. Even President Reagan, who was criticized by his political opponents as being too old to be President, made jokes exaggerating his age. However, it is not polite for another person to do this. Most people will resent being **kidded*** about their shortcomings.

<> A fat man was trying unsuccessfully to get through the **turnstile*** at the subway station. A man passing him watched for a while and then said,
"Why don't you try sideways?"
"Because I don't have a sideways."

(Why don't you try sideways? = Turn and try to enter side first instead of front first.)

<> A fat man was sitting next to a thin man on the bus. The thin man was annoyed because the fat man was taking up most of the seat.
"They ought to charge by weight on these buses," said the thin man.
"Well, if they did," replied the fat man, "you'd have to walk. It wouldn't pay them to stop for you."

81

Dieting seems to be a a national **hobby***. Almost half our population will be on a weight-restricting diet at some time in their lives. Years ago, it was fashionable to be a little **chubby***. Being fat was a sign of wealth and social distinction. Among the poor, extra fat on children meant that they would have a better chance of living through a depression or **crop*** failure. Now, being fat is a cause of anxiety. Being lean is considered healthier and more desirable.

<> A very large lady finished her dinner in a restaurant and asked for dessert. "I'd like a banana split, with three scoops of ice cream, hot chocolate sauce, walnuts, and whipped cream."
"Very good, Madame," said the waiter. "Would you like a cherry on top?"
"Heavens, no! I'm on a diet!"

<> "How did your wife make out with that new diet?"
"Fine, she disappeared completely last week."

American men are very **preoccupied*** with the problem of losing their hair. **Tonics***, massages, vitamins, and special shampoos fill the shelves in the drugstores. Nothing seems to work. If someone could invent a sure cure for **restoring*** hair, he would be a millionaire. All we have is humor to lessen the anxiety.

<> Bald-headed man at the barber shop: I should get a **discount***, because I don't have much hair for you to cut.
Barber: Sir, half the price is for cutting your hair, the other half is for looking for it.

83

<> "How did you lose all your hair?"
"By worrying."
"About what?"
"Losing my hair."

<> Barber to child: How would you like your
hair cut?
Child: Like my Daddy's.
Barber: And how is that?
Child: With a hole in the middle.

<> A very fat and ugly woman had a pet duck
that she carried with her under her arm. One day
she walked into a **barroom***. A drunk was standing
near the door. The drunk looked at her, and then
looked at the duck.
"Where in the world did you get that pig?"
asked the drunk.
"I beg your pardon," said the fat lady. "You
are obviously drunk. This happens to be a <u>duck.</u>"
"And I beg <u>your</u> pardon," said the drunk. "<u>I</u>
was talking to the duck."

("Pig" is a very **derogatory*** slang term for an
ugly, unattractive woman.)

A **handicap*** is not funny to the person who has one.
There are many jokes about the difficulties of deaf, **dumb***,
(mute) or blind people, but they are not told in the presence of
someone with such a handicap.

<> Three **deaf*** ladies were riding on a bus.
All the windows were open and the air was blowing all
around. "Oh my, isn't it windy!" said the first one.
"No, it isn't Wednesday, it's Thursday," said
the second lady.
"Yes, I'm thirsty, too," said the third. "Let's
all get off and have some lemonade."

(The humor is based on the fact that each woman has

misunderstood what the others said.)

<> A man was **bragging*** to his friend about his new hearing aid. "It is the latest, and most expensive model. I paid over two thousand dollars for this hearing aid. With this hearing aid, I can hear the softest whisper across a room, and I can hear the birds singing in trees a block away."
"That's great," said his friend. "What kind is it?"
The first man looked at his watch and replied, "It's four-thirty."

(His wonderful expensive hearing aid didn't help him hear the question correctly. He thought the question was, What <u>time</u> is it?)

<> A man who was **hard-of-hearing*** was lost in a strange city. He stopped a man on the street to ask for directions.
"Pardon me, sir, can you tell me how to get to Adams Street?"
"What's that? I didn't hear you. I'm a little deaf."
"I beg your pardon?"
"I said, I'm a little deaf."
"You don't say. I'm deaf, too."
"That's too bad. Now, what was it you wanted?"
"Can you tell me how to get to Adams Street?"
"Sure. Go straight down this street for four blocks, then turn right. Go three more blocks and you'll be there."
"That's Adams Street, is it?"
"Oh, no. Excuse me. I thought you said Adams Street."
"No, I said Adams Street."
"Never heard of it. Sorry, I can't help you."

Drunks

Drinking is a serious problem in America, and the drunk is the butt of a lot of humor. The stereotyped drunk is unreliable*, clumsy*, confused and accident-prone*. His speech slurs*. We laugh at the behavior of the drunk, because we too, have sometimes been unreliable, clumsy, and confused. Alcohol abuse* causes accidents, wrecks homes, and destroys marriages. We make jokes and laugh at the drunk, because sometimes it hurts too much to cry.

<> A drunk walks up to a **parking meter*** and puts in a dime. The pointer goes up to 60. "Gee," says the drunk. "I lost a hundred pounds."

<> A young woman who had been married for only three months was complaining to her friend about her husband's drinking.

"If you knew he drank, then why did you marry him?"

"I didn't know he drank," said the young woman, "until one night he came home **sober*!**"

<> "My wife has a very annoying habit," said the drunk to the bartender.

"What's that?" he asked.

"She stays up every night until 2 or 3 o'clock in the morning."

"What in the world is she doing up at that hour?"

"Waiting for me to come home."

<> A drunk was walking home from the **saloon*** and took a **shortcut*** through the **cemetery***. He was **staggering*** around and fell into a freshly dug **grave***. He tried to climb out but the sides were too **steep***. He called for help, but no one could hear him. Night came, and it became very chilly.

"I'm c-c-c-cold!" he said over and over. "I'm c-c-c-cold."

After a long time, another drunk came walking through the cemetery and he heard the first one crying. He walked over to the grave and saw the first drunk with his arms wrapped around himself trying to keep warm.

"It's no wonder you're cold," said the second

drunk. "You've gone and kicked off all your dirt."

(A restless child might kick his covers off the bed during the night. The second drunk thought that the drunk in the grave was a dead man who had kicked off the dirt that was covering him.)

<> A man bought a valuable **grandfather clock*** at an **auction***, but there were no delivery trucks available, so he decided to carry it home by himself. He lifted it onto his shoulder and struggled the six blocks to his building. Just as he was getting near his house, a drunk staggered out of a bar and bumped into him, knocking the man down. The grandfather clock fell down in a crash, and broke into several pieces.

The man was furious. "Why don't you watch where you're going?" he shouted at the drunk.

"And why don't you jush wear a watch like everyone elsh?" asked the drunk.

(jush = just; elsh = else [slurred talk])

<> The owner of a bar got a phone call at three a.m. "What time does your bar open in the morning?" asked a man in a drunken voice.

"At nine o'clock."

At five a.m. he got another call and the same voice asked, "What time did you say your bar opens?"

"I told you, at nine o'clock."

Two hours later the phone rang again with the same question. By this time, the owner was losing his patience. "Look, there is no way you can get into the bar before nine o'clock."

"Get in? Who wants to get in? I want to get out!"

Exercises

I Vocabulary

Choose the best word to complete the following sentences:

parking meter   crop   clumsy

unreliable   discount   shortcut

turnstile

1. Jones' Department Store is having a big sale. There is a 25%

   _____ on all winter coats and sweaters.

2.   Freezing weather, insects and too much rain ruined the
   apple _____ this year.

3. Put a quarter in the _____ so
   you can leave your car here for one hour.

4. You have to put a coin in the _____ before
   it will turn and let you enter.

5. A person who does not keep promises is
   _____.

6. Betsy was so _____ , she couldn't put
   on her coat without dropping her hat and gloves, and knocking
   over a lamp.

7. Bob was in a hurry to get home, so he took a

   _____ through the park.

II Match the word with the meaning:

1. cemetery_____   A. drunken speech

2. stagger_____   B. bar, a place to drink beer

3. saloon_____   C. fat

4. sober_____   D. not drunk

5. chubby_____   E. place where the dead are buried

6. slur_____   F. hard-of-hearing

7. deaf_____   G. drunken walking

8. magnify _____   H. make larger

III Discussion

1. Are there many overweight people in your country? What is the attitude towards fat?

2. Are jokes about people's defects commonly told? What do you think of such jokes?

3. Is drinking alcohol a problem in your country? Are drunks the butt of many jokes? Can you tell any?

CHAPTER TWELVE: How Dumb Can You Get?

Are any of us as smart as we would like to be? Probably not. But we can feel a whole lot smarter when we exaggerate the stupidity of others. It's harmless fun, too.

<> "This match won't light."
"What's wrong with it?"
"I don't know. It worked all right five minutes ago."

<> "The moon is more useful than the sun."
"Why is that?"
"Well, the moon gives light at night when we need it to see, and the sun shines in the daytime when we don't need it."

<> Two moving men were struggling for hours with a huge piano in a doorway. They pushed and tugged and finally they were all tired out, but it wouldn't move.
"Let's give up," said the first man. "We're just never going to get it in."
"Get it in!" said the second man. "And all this time I thought we were trying to get it out!"

<> "So-and-so* is so dumb, he has T.G.I.F. written on all his shoes."
"What for?"
"Toes Go In First."

(T.G.I.F. is an abbreviation that usually means "Thank God It's Friday," said by workers or students after a tiring week.)

<> Two carpenters were building a house. One of them was hammering nails into the side boards. He examined each nail before he used it, and he threw most of them away.

The other carpenter asked him why he was throwing away so many nails.

"They're no good. Some **dummy*** made them backwards. The **heads*** are on the wrong side of the nail," said the first carpenter.

"You're the dummy," said the second carpenter. "Don't throw those away, those nails are for the other side of the house."

<> Two boys were on a bicycle-built-for-two. They had a very hard time going up a steep hill, but they finally got to the top.

"Whew," said the first boy. "I didn't think we'd ever make it."

"Well, I helped," said the second boy. "I kept on the brakes on so we wouldn't roll back down."

<> Two **dopes*** were out fishing. They were pulling in a lot of fish, and were very happy about it. "Let's come back tomorrow to this same spot," said one. "I'll mark the bottom of the boat with a piece of chalk."

"You dumb ox! That won't work. How do you know we'll get the same boat?"

<> A dope was carrying a box and he met his friend. "Guess how many chickens I have in this box, and I'll give you both of them," he said.

("Both" = two, giving away the secret.)

<> A dope comes home to find another man kissing his wife. He opens a drawer, pulls out a

gun, and points it at his own head.
His wife laughs.
"Don't laugh," he says. "You're next."

<> Two men went into business together. They
bought a truck and drove down south to Georgia and
bought a load of watermelons for one dollar each.
They drove the truckload of melons to New York and
sold them for one dollar each. When they got done
counting their money, they found that they had not
made any profit.
"What do you think the problem is?" asked the
first.
They thought and thought a long time. "What
we need is a bigger truck," said the second.

<> A man walked into a **deli*** with a huge
two-quart **thermos.*** "Hey, can I get **coffee-to-go*** in
this?"
"Sure you can," says the clerk. "How would
you like it?"
"One regular; two light, no sugar; one black; .
. . "

(When asking for coffee, the customer tells the waiter
whether he wants milk and sugar. "Regular" = coffee with milk
and sugar. "Light" = extra milk. "Black" = no milk. The
customer in this joke (who is buying coffee for three or four
co-workers or friends) is so stupid he doesn't realize that all the
coffee will be mixed together in the single large thermos.)

<> "I had a terrible train trip. All the way
from New York to Buffalo, I rode backwards. I was
sick to my stomach."
"Why didn't you ask the person in the seat
facing you to change seats?"
"I thought of that, but there wasn't anyone
there."

Jokes about stupidity have been around for a long time.
Recently, these old jokes have been re-told using members of
ethnic groups* as the butts. See CHAPTER THIRTEEN.

94

City People

Ninety percent of the population of the United States now lives in **urban*** areas. Many of these city people have no contact with nature. When these city people visit the **rural*** areas, they are in another world. In the stereotype, they feel superior to the farmer, while being **ignorant*** of some very simple facts of life.

<> The visitor from the city was annoying the farmer with his many questions. He pointed to an animal in the field. "Why doesn't that cow have any horns?" he wanted to know.

"Well," said the farmer. "There are three reasons why a cow may not have horns. Some cows are born without horns. Some cows lose their horns if they are sick. And we cut the horns off some cows to keep them from hurting people. But the reason that <u>that cow</u> there doesn't have any horns, is that <u>that cow</u> is a <u>horse</u>."

<> A tobacco farmer was showing a city lady around his **plantation.*** "These are tobacco plants. They're in **full bloom*** now."

"Oh, that's wonderful. When will the cigarettes be **ripe***?"

<> A tourist from the city was driving through the country and he wasn't sure that he was on the right road. He stopped to ask a farmer for directions.

"Which way is it to Route 95?" he asked.

"Don't know," said the farmer.

"Well, will this road take me to New Hampshire?"

"Don't know," said the farmer again.

The tourist was annoyed. "Don't you know ANYTHING?"

"Well," said the farmer. "I know <u>I</u> ain't lost!"

Exercises

I Vocabulary

Choose the best word to complete the sentences:

light   ripe   full bloom

thermos   deli   plantations   head

1. Hit the nail on the _____.

2. When will the peaches be _____ enough to eat?

3. I take a _____ full of hot coffee to work every morning.

4. You can buy sliced ham and cheese at the _____.

5. In April, the cherry trees are in _____ in Washington.

6. Cotton grows on large _____ in the South.

7. Put in extra milk. I like my coffee _____, with no sugar.

II Discussion

1. Are any of these jokes similar to jokes in your country?

2. Where do most of the people in your country live, in cities or in rural areas?

CHAPTER THIRTEEN: Regional and Ethnic* Jokes

Americans come from many different national backgrounds. We are **enriched*** by this variety; it is one of the greatest sources of America's strength.

The major ethnic groups in the U.S. are people of English or German **background*** (sometimes called the White **Anglo-Saxon*** Protestants (WASPs). Other groups are "**minority***" groups (because there are fewer of them). They are the Blacks, Hispanics, and people of Irish, Jewish, Italian, and Russian backgrounds. In addition there are smaller groups of Greeks, Polish, Swedes, Dutch, Hungarians, Scottish, French, Native Americans (Indians), Norwegians, Chinese, Japanese, Koreans, Vietnamese, Arabs, and countless others.

Individuals from every race, color, language group, and ethnic group have contributed to the growth of America. Some basic ideals of our society are: liberty and justice for all; all men (and women) are created equal; this is a land of equal opportunity; an individual should be judged by his character and not by his race, religion, or ethnic background.

These high ideals are found in our schoolbooks and in our laws, but not in our jokes.

Lack of understanding can arise between groups of people whose appearance, customs, or values are different. Competition, jealousy, resentment, fear, and anxiety also exist between groups. Humor is one way of attacking another group in a playful way. By telling a funny story that makes another group appear inferior, the teller makes himself and the listeners appear superior. "Aren't we lucky we're not as low, stupid, dirty, stingy, selfish, smelly, ugly, poor, or sexually perverted as THOSE OTHERS!" All of this is really on an unconscious level. People don't generally analyze the reason they find things funny.

Some ethnic jokes are gentle, and almost everyone will enjoy them. Others are unkind, and even **vicious***. It is difficult for a foreign student to tell them apart.

Stereotypes of the different racial, regional and ethnic groups exist. If you are aware of the stereotype, you have a better chance of understanding some of the jokes. Remember: Stereotypes are often totally false. It is impossible to generalize accurately about a whole group of people. Stereotypes represent lazy thinking.

Often a member of a group will enjoy telling jokes that have his own group as the butt. Some ethnic jokes are interchangeable--that is, whether it's told as an Irish joke or a Polish joke or an Italian joke, it may still be funny. Students at one college may tell "ethnic" jokes about the students at a **rival***
college.

The most frequent stereotype of another ethnic group is that members of that group are stupid. Many of the jokes about stupidity in CHAPTER TWELVE may also be told as ethnic jokes. Instead of saying "three men", for example, the joke teller says "three Irishmen" or, "three Polish guys" or "a Norwegian, a Finn and a Swede," "an Italian, a Puerto Rican and a Black," and so forth.

Ethnic humor may **ease*** the relationships between groups, or make tensions worse. Our advice to the foreign student: Beware of telling an ethnic joke about a group that is not your own. Do not tell ethnic jokes to people whose backgrounds you do not know. Jokes that are anti-Semitic (anti-Jewish) or anti-Black can be especially **offensive***. Many people never tell ethnic jokes, because they feel these jokes encourage **prejudice***.

In spite of this, ethnic jokes are the fastest-growing kind of jokes today. Most of them are told in a spirit of fun, with no **malice*** intended, and most people enjoy them. It is not the purpose of this book to tell you what you should think is funny. However, it is necessary to point out that there are social dangers in telling ethnic jokes.

Regional "ethnic" jokes

"Hillbilly" is a word used to describe a person who lives in the hills and has never gone to school. Hillbillies are stereotyped as uneducated, whiskey-loving, and **barefoot***. They wear long beards, carry shotguns and make moonshine (illegal whiskey) in their backyards. They are suspicious of strangers and will shoot anyone **trespassing*** on their land.

<> A tourist saw a hillbilly sitting on hisbroken-down porch with a jug next to him. "What do you do around these parts?" the tourist asked.

"We just drink whiskey and hunt," was the answer.

"Oh. What do you hunt for?"

"Whiskey."

<> A hillbilly told his wife that he had learned to write. He handed her a piece of paper with marks on it.

"What does it say?" his wife wanted to know.

"Don't know. Ain't* learned to read yet."

(here, ain't = I haven't)

Texas is a big state, and everything in Texas is done in a big way. The stereotype of a Texan is that he is over six feet tall, is very wealthy, drives a very long powerful car and lives in **luxury*** on a very, very large ranch.

A Texan was **bragging*** about the size of his
ranch*. "I get in my car and leave my house at six
in the morning and arrive at the main gate to my
ranch at two o'clock in the afternoon," he said.
"That's funny," said his bored listener. "I had
a car just like that once."

(The listener thinks that the car was slow, but the Texan
meant that his ranch was very, very large.)

<> "Did you hear about the Texan who bought
a set of blocks for his child to play with?"
"What's so special about that?"
"The blocks were 45th Street, 46th Street, 47th
Street . . ."

IMPORTANT NOTE: In different sections of the United
States, different ethnic groups are the butts of jokes. We do not
wish to encourage negative ethnic stereotypes. For these
reasons, the following jokes will not mention any specific ethnic
group. We have replaced specific ethnic groups such as Italian,
Polish, Irish, Ukrainian, Norwegian, Puerto Rican, Black, etc.,
with the general term, "Ethnic."

<> How can you tell the **bride*** at an Ethnic
wedding?
She's the one in a clean T-shirt.

(The ethnic group is exaggeratedly dirty and poorly
dressed. Only the bride is clean for this special occasion, but
she has no wedding gown. Every one else is wearing a dirty
T-shirt to the wedding.)

<> How can you break an Ethnic's finger?
Punch him in the nose.

(These people are always picking their noses in
public.)

100

<> Who came in first in the Ethnic beauty contest?
No one.

(There are no beautiful young women in this ethnic group.)

<> Then there was the Ethnic factory worker who had used up all his sick days, so he called in dead.

(sick days = a certain number of days when a worker may stay home from work because of illness, and not lose any pay. This person called his boss to say he couldn't come to work because he was dead. He must be very dumb to think the boss will believe him.)

<> How many Ethnics does it take to make popcorn?
Five: One to hold the pan and four to shake the stove.

(Popcorn is generally made by putting dried corn in a frying pan and shaking it over a hot flame until the corn pops.)

<> Where do Ethnics hide their money?
Under the soap.

(They are so dirty, they never use soap, so the money will not be discovered accidentally.)

<> An Ethnic in the big city was attacked by a mugger*. He fought back bravely for a long time. The mugger was hurt and bleeding when he finally grabbed the Ethnic's wallet. The mugger looked in the wallet. There were only four dollars in it.
"Tell me," said the mugger. "Why did you fight so hard when you only had four dollars in your wallet?"

101

"I thought you were after the $600 in my shoe," said the Ethnic.

(The Ethnic person is so dumb, he has just told the mugger where he had hidden $600. If he had kept quiet, the mugger would not have known that he had more money.)

<> There's a garbage strike in Ethnic Land. No deliveries for three days.

<> What do you call a pretty girl in Ethnic Land?
A tourist.

(As in the joke about the beauty contest--there are no pretty girls in Ethnic Land...only the ones that come in temporarily as tourists.)

Some ethnic jokes rely on the use of dialect, or a special foreign accent to increase the laugh value.

(Part of the humor in the next joke is from the use of an Italian accent. Italian words all end in vowels, so when an Italian speaks English, he tends to add a vowel sound to the end of words that don't end in vowels. eg. Legga = leg or legs, jumpa = jump, deafa = **deaf***. The "th" sound is difficult for many foreigners. Widda = with a.)

<> An Italian scientist was conducting experiments on frogs. He draws a white chalk line on the floor and puts a frog down on this line. He says, "Jumpa." The frog jumps five feet. So he writes in his book, 'Frogga widda four legga, he jumpa five-a feeta.'
He takes a knife and cuts one leg off the frog and says to the frog, "Jumpa!" The frog jumps three feet. So he writes in his book, 'Frogga widda three legga, he jumpa three feeta.'
He cuts one more leg off the frog and says, "Jumpa!" The frog jumps one foot. He writes in his book, 'Frogga widda two legga, he jumpa one-a foota.'
He cuts another leg off, and the frog jumps 6

102

inches. So he writes in his book, 'Frogga widda one legga, he jumpa sixa incha.'

Then he cuts the last leg off the frog. "Jumpa!" he says, but the frog doesn't jump. "Jumpa!" he says again, but the frog doesn't jump. "Jumpa! he shouts. Nothing. So he writes down in his book, 'Frogga widda no legga, he deafa.'

<> A Japanese businessman went to the eye doctor for an examination.

"You have a cataract," said the doctor.

"No," said the Japanese gentleman. "I have a Rincoln."

(Japanese speakers of English have difficulty with the sounds of "l" and "r," often confusing them. Cataract = an eye disease. The Japanese thought the doctor said "Cadillac" (an expensive car). He replied that he had a Lincoln (another expensive car), but, having difficulty with the "l" sound, pronounced it "Rincoln."

104

Exercises

I Vocabulary

Match these words with the correct meaning:

enrich   Anglo-Saxon   minority   barefoot

trespass   luxury   offensive

malice   mugger   ethnic group

1. Make richer or more complete _____

2. To enter someone's house or land without permission _____

3. A desire to hurt other people _____

4. Wealth, richness _____

5. Insulting, causing anger _____

6. Without shoes _____

7. English _____

8. A group of people with a common culture, language, religon or national background _____

9. The old woman was beaten by a _____ who then took her pocketbook.

II Discussion

1. Are there various ethnic groups in your country? Are all groups treated equally under the law? Are there serious tensions among the groups? Are there ethnic jokes about them? What characteristics of the ethnic groups are stereotyped in the jokes?

2. How do you feel about ethnic jokes when they are told about your ethnic group?

3. In your opinion, do ethnic jokes increase or decrease good feelings between different groups of people?

CHAPTER FOURTEEN: Progress and Problems

If you pick up a newspaper, or watch the news on TV, you will learn of many problems in the world today. Some of these problems have always been with us: crime, war, disease, hunger, **poverty***, and **corruption.***

Other problems seem to be new. They come from new inventions, new styles, and new ways of doing things. Modern art and music seem **unintelligible*** to the average person. Technology has advanced faster than people's ability to understand or control it.

Our standard of living has improved, but we pay for it in many ways. The automobile and the airplane have brought us better and faster ways of going places. But they have also brought us air **pollution***, accidents, and **traffic jams.*** Television has brought entertainment to millions, but has reduced our ability to entertain ourselves. Computers have simplified many jobs, but they have removed the human contact and personal attention we all need.

Today we have chemical poisons in our food, street crime, **economic recessions***, **inflation***, high taxes, **acid rain***, **fuel*** shortages, dangers from **nuclear reactors***, the threat of nuclear war and the **extermination*** of the human race. We need more than humor to **combat*** these problems, and some days the news is so bad, nothing can make us laugh. As soon as a **crisis*** is over, however, there are new jokes going around to help us relieve the tension and go back to business as usual.

<> A **shipwrecked*** sailor had spent five years alone a **deserted*** island. At last he saw a ship sail near his island. He made a fire to signal the ship. The ship stopped and sent a small boat to the island to rescue the sailor. On the small boat was a pile of the latest newspapers, with the world news.
"Read these newspapers," said his rescuer, "and see if you still want to be rescued."

<> "Nowadays you have to be very careful of what you eat," said Mack.
"Is that so?" said Jack.
"Yes. I have made a thorough study of the matter and I don't eat anything with **preservatives*** or **artificial*** coloring."
"Really!"
"I stay away from meat from animals that were fed chemicals with their **grain.*** I never buy vegetables or fruits that have been sprayed with **pesticides*.**"
"So now that you are so careful about your food, how do you feel?"
"Hungry."

<> "I've invented a computer that is almost human."
"How is that?"
"When it makes a mistake it blames it on another computer."

<> On a dark street of New York, a young man walks up to an older man. "Say, have you seen a policeman around here?" he asks.
"No I haven't," says the older man.
"All right then, this is a **stickup*. Hand over*** your wallet."

<> A gas station had this sign out front: We collect taxes: state, **federal*** and local. We also sell gas as a **sideline*.**

(The owners of the gas station are being **sarcastic*.** A big part of the price of gas goes for taxes. The owners must fill out many papers to send the proper amount of tax to the town, the state, and the national government. They are exaggerating the amount of time that it takes to do this, and say that they sell gas only as an extra, after they have done the work as tax collectors.)

107

<> "I've invented something to allow people to see through walls."

"Wonderful! What are you going to call it?"

"A Window."

<> A man is looking at a blank **canvas*** in an art museum. The artist is near him. "What does this painting represent?"

"It's a cow, eating grass."

"Where is the grass?"

"The cow has eaten it."

"Well, I don't see the cow. Where is the cow?"

"Oh, you don't think she's dumb enough to stay around after she'd eaten all the grass, do you?"

<> A man consulted a fortune teller. She read his **palm*** and said, "You'll be poor and unhappy until you are forty."

"And after that?" asked the man.

"You'll still be poor, but by that time, you'll be used to it."

<> The service from the telephone company is getting worse and worse. Why, the other day, I called Information to find out what number I had to dial to get Information, and the operator told me I'd have to call Information.

<> Minnie: Hey Molly, did you see the moon last night?
Molly: What channel?

(channel = TV channel)

<> In the waiting room three **expectant*** fathers were **pacing*** the floor.
"This is a bad time to become a father," said the first one. "I just lost my job."
"It's worse for me," said the second man. "I was on my vacation."
"That's nothing." said the third. "I was on my honeymoon."

Fear of Flying

<>"Did you hear about the man who took a bus to California because he was afraid of flying?"
"No, what happened?"
"A plane crashed into his bus."

<> A brand new airplane was taking off for the first time. The seats were very comfortable, and the passengers were in a good **mood***. When the plane was 30,000 feet above the ground the usual message came over the loudspeaker from the captain:
"Ladies and gentlemen, I'd like to welcome you aboard flight number 235 of Fly-High Airlines. This is the very first all-computer crew ever to fly an airplane. There is no need for a pilot or co-pilot, since the entire flight has been programmed to provide you with every possible comfort and luxury

109

while you travel at the speed of sound across the
ocean to Europe. All navigating decisions will be
made by computer, and absolutely nothing can go
wrong. . . go wrong. . . go wrong . . . go wrong .
. ."

<> An Ethnic is flying to Europe on a
four-engine plane. Everything is going along nicely
when there comes a message from the captain over the
loudspeaker.
"This is your captain speaking. We have had a
little difficulty. One of our engines has broken
down. There will be an hour delay in reaching
Europe."
A half hour later, the pilot gets on the
loudspeaker again, and says, "Ladies and gentlemen,
I'm sorry to tell you that two of our engines are now
broken. There will be a three-hour delay in reaching
Europe."
And in another while, the captain again
announces, "Ladies and gentlemen, now three of our
engines are out. There will be a five-hour delay in
reaching Europe."
The Ethnic looks at the man sitting next to him
in disgust. "What luck. And if the last engine goes
out, we'll be up here all day!"

The air controllers are very busy people who work in the
control towers at airports to give directions to planes that are
taking off and landing. Sometimes they hear some strange
messages from pilots. Like this one:

<> "Pilot to control tower! Pilot to control
tower! I'm coming in. Please give me landing
instructions! Hurry!"
"Control tower to pilot. Control tower to pilot.
Why are you yelling so loud?"
"Pilot to control tower! Pilot to control tower!
I don't have a radio."

110

Exercises

I Vocabulary

Match the words with the correct definitions:

1. Combat _____   A. state of being poor

2. pollution _____   B. impossible to understand

3. poverty _____   C. mental health

4. unintellibible _____ D. not natural

5. palm _____   E. poison used to kill insects

6. sanity _____   F. walk back and forth

7. artificial _____   G. the front of the hand

8. pesticide _____   H. give possession of something to another

9. pace _____   I. dirt in air or water

10. hand over _____   J. fight

II Discussion

1. Pick up a copy of today's paper. What problems do the news stories tell of? Which problems are a concern to you? What problems in your country are not a problem in the United States?

CHAPTER FIFTEEN: Work Jokes and Formula Jokes

Unless we are born rich, we all have to face the problem of earning a living*. A person who is happy at the work he or she does is considered very lucky. Today, modern technology and labor-saving devices* make life a lot easier for most Americans. We have many hours for leisure* activities, such as sports, games, TV, and traveling. Work and laziness, bosses and employees have become the butts of jokes.

<> I love work. I could sit and watch it for hours.

(i.e., admire it, but not do it.)

<> Boss: The other workers are carrying fifty pounds of stuff on each trip and you're carrying only twenty-five. How do you explain that?
Worker: Oh, they're just too lazy to make two trips, the way I do.

<> A new waiter was so clumsy he was continually breaking glasses. The owner called him in to his office. "You have broken more dishes in one week than your week's salary can pay for. What do you suggest is the solution for this problem?"
"Could you give me a raise*?"

(i.e., then the waiter could afford to pay for the broken dishes, but he probably won't stop breaking them.)

<> A young man applies for a job.
"This is an important position you are applying for," says the boss. "We need someone who can

112

handle responsibility. Are you a responsible person?"
"Oh yes, sir. I'm very responsible," the applicant says. "In my last job, whenever something went wrong I was responsible."

(Responsible here has two meanings. The boss wants someone who is capable of being a manager. The applicant has a history of being the person who caused problems.)

<> Boss to the new worker: Did the supervisor explain what to do?
New worker: Oh, yes, sir. He said to wake him up when I saw you coming.

(The supervisor is very lazy, but doesn't want the boss to find out that he sleeps on the job.)

<> The boss was showing a new employee around the office.
"How many people work here?" asked the new man.
"About half of them," said the boss.

(i.e. The other half of the people are so lazy they do no work at all. The new employee really wanted to know the number of employees in the office, but the boss interprets the question as, "How many of these people actually do the work they are paid to do.")

<> Bookstore clerk: This book will cut your work in half.
Customer: Great, I'll take two.

<> Boss to secretary: Miss Smith, you have fallen behind in your work again. If you can't work any faster, I'll have to get a new secretary.
Secretary: Oh, thank you, Mr. Jones. I could use the help.

(The boss means that he will **fire*** her and find a new

secretary. The secretary is so stupid, she thinks the boss will **hire*** an assistant for her.)

<> How do you do it? You've only been with the company two weeks, and already you're a month behind in your work.

Light Bulb Jokes

Occasionally a new joke inspires other jokes of a similar nature. The "light bulb" jokes are an example of this. The first one appeared in 1980 and soon there were dozens and dozens of light bulb jokes. Many of them are ethnic jokes. By <u>extreme exaggeration</u>, they demonstrate stereotyped attitudes towards different ethnic, political, or occupational groups. New jokes are created using the same formula, or pattern.

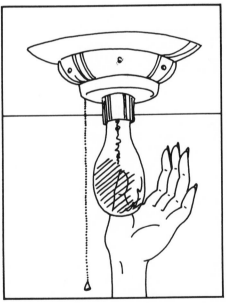

<> How many Ethnics does it take to change a light bulb?
Four. One to hold the light bulb and three to turn the ladder he's standing on.

(i.e., the Ethnics are so dumb that they cannot solve simple problems; they make a job much more difficult than it is.)

<> How many WASP's does it take to change a light bulb?
Two: one to call the electrician and one to mix the **martinis***.

114

(The WASP's are imagined to be so rich that they hire someone to do even the easiest of jobs that require physical work. This small occasion is also a reason for them to have a sociable alcoholic drink.)

<> How many Jewish Mothers does it take to change a light bulb?
"Don't worry about me, I'll just sit here in the dark."

(This is said slowly, with a sigh, as though the speaker were in pain. The Jewish Mother (caricature of all mothers) puts herself in a situation (in the dark, and unable to see) that will cause her children to feel guilty.)

<> How many Republicans does it take to change a light bulb?
Three: One to change the light bulb and two to complain about how much better the old one was.

(The Republican Party is more conservative than the Democratic Party.)

<> How many psychiatrists does it take to change a light bulb?
One, but the light bulb must really want to change.

(There is a play on the word "change." Psychiatrists explain the failure of their treatment with some patients by saying that the patients did not really <u>want</u> to change their behavior.)

<> How many Japanese does it take to change a light bulb?
Three. One to change the light bulb, one to hold his camera, and one to take a picture of him doing it.

115

(Japanese tourists always seem to have cameras around their necks.)

<> How many organized laborers does it take to change a light bulb?
Seven: One to get the ladder. One to get the light bulb. One to hold the ladder. One to climb the ladder and unscrew the old light bulb. One to take the old light bulb from him. One to hand him a new light bulb. One to hold the ladder while he climbs down.

(Organized laborers = union workers. New machinery now can do the jobs of many workers, and employers save money by firing the workers who are no longer needed. Some strong unions have demanded that their employers keep jobs for as many workers as possible, even though their jobs are unnecessary.)

Good News-Bad News

Occasionally a new joke form is developed and suddenly there seem to be many new jokes using this form. The "good news--bad news" jokes are an example. A person announces some good news, that should make the listener happy. But the bad news that comes with it is absolutely horrible, and takes away any pleasure the good news could have brought.

<> Good news: You have just won a million dollars in the **lottery***.
Bad news: I'm with the Internal Revenue Service.

(The I. R. S. is the national agency that collects income taxes. There will be very little money left, after taxes.)

<> Good news: Your boyfriend just broke the Olympic diving record for the triple **somersault*** from the high diving board.
Bad news: There was no water in the pool at the time.

<> Good news: Captain, land is only two miles away. Bad news: It's straight down.

(By addressing the listener as "Captain," the location of the joke is obviously on a ship. The location of the land is the bottom of the ocean. These sailors are lost.)

<> Good news: I've just invented the light bulb.
Bad news: I can't get it to ring.

(The inventor has confused the light bulb with the telephone.)

<> Good news: I just heard that the President is going to China.
The bad news: He's coming back.

(This joke may be told about any disliked famous person who is about to take a trip to some far-away place.)

The bad news may be announced first. It tells of some very awful situation. The good news is something very unimportant and does not help the situation at all.

<> The dictator of a very poor country got on television to speak to his people. "My fellow citizens. Tonight I have some good news and some bad news to report. First the bad news: The **crops*** have failed and there is nothing to eat but **lizards***.
Now the good news: There aren't enough lizards to **go around***."

<> Bad news: Your car just slipped its brakes and drove off the **cliff*** into the **Grand Canyon.***
Good news: It got 38 miles to the gallon on the way down.

(i.e., good gas mileage, proving that it is a very economical car to drive.)

118

<> **Masochist*** to **sadist***: I have good news and bad news. The good news is, there's a lot of bad news.

(A masochist is a person who gets pleasure from pain. A sadist is a person who enjoys giving pain to others.)

<> Bad news: My son married the cleaning lady.
Good news: She does windows.

(Today's houseworkers such as cleaning ladies may refuse to do some of the more difficult and tedious jobs such as washing windows. A cleaning lady who "does windows" is considered exceptional, and is highly valued by her employers.)

Exercises

I Vocabulary

Choose the best word to complete the following sentences:

masochist   leisure   site   labor-saving devices
raise   fire   hire   somersault   lottery
sadist   cliff   go around   lizard

1. A _____ enjoys being hit or beaten, while a
_____ enjoys giving pain to others.

2. A vacuum cleaner, a micro-wave oven, a washing machine and
an electric dishwasher are all examples of _____
_____.

3. Mrs. Clark wanted to _____ a cleaning lady to
do the laundry, make the beds, and wash the floors.

4. The new cleaning lady broke so many glasses and other
valuable things that Mrs. Clark had to _____ her.

5. My salary is very low. I hope I get a _____ in pay
soon.

6. A _____ is a four-legged animal covered with
scales. It looks like a small alligator.

7. The average person works eight hours, sleeps eight hours,
spends four hours on eating, dressing and personal care, and
has four hours of _____ every day.

8. The child did _____s down the hill,
rolling head over heels, again and again until she reached the
bottom.

9. My friend was climbing a mountain, but he fell off a
_____ and broke his leg.

10. There were ten apples for ten children, just enough to
_____.

121

11. Dick bought a _____ ticket. He hopes to win some money.

12. The builders have chosen the _____ for the new school. It will be on Market Street.

II Discussion

1. Do you have a job now? Is it boring or interesting? Do you hope to change your job some day? Is it easy to change jobs in your country?

2. Is there a lot of unemployment in your country? Is there unemployment insurance? What is the attitude towards work? Are unions strong in your country?

3. Do people tell light bulb jokes in your country? Good News - Bad News jokes? Can you tell one?

CHAPTER SIXTEEN: How to Tell a Joke

Joke telling is an art. Some people get others to laugh quite naturally, without ever thinking about how they do it. Other people find that they need some **tips*** to help them improve their joke-telling skills.

If you would like to become a better joke teller, and get more laughs from your listeners, ask yourself these questions:

Do I understand the joke?

Many people have tried to get laughs from jokes they read or have heard other people tell, without really understanding why they are funny. Tell jokes that you have laughed at yourself.

If the joke is one you know in your own language, be sure it does not have the kind of punch line that is "lost in translation."

Do I know the joke?

Your audience will not be eager to listen to you again if you tell the beginning of a joke and then forget the punch line! Be sure you can remember the whole joke before you begin.

Practice telling the joke in front of a mirror. Get the wording right, memorize it so that there will be no unnecessary hesitation. Practice on one person before you tell jokes to groups.

If you have trouble remembering jokes that are told to you, don't be ashamed of taking notes when you hear a good joke.

Do I know my audience?

Is this joke a good joke to tell this particular person or group of people? Will anyone be offended?

Who is the butt of the joke?

What happens to the butt, and will the audience be glad for it?

Mothers-in-law may not see anything funny in mother-in-law jokes. Religious or ethnic jokes may offend members of those religions or ethnic groups that are mentioned. A single woman may not see the humor in a joke about husbands that a married woman sees.

Students who eat in the school cafeteria will probably find jokes about cafeteria food funny. The cafeteria's cooks and workers who are doing their best to prepare and serve the food will be less amused.

A male, telling a joke to a group of "liberated*" women, should not expect them to find his jokes about women drivers or dumb housewives funny.

Is this the right time to tell this joke?

Jokes are funnier when people have the time to relax and listen to them. Often these times are when you are relaxing after meals, or at parties. There are other times that jokes might not be welcome. The teller must be sensitive to the listener's feelings.

Why is the wording the way it is?

No two people tell a joke using the exact same words or the exact same order of words. But some variations of telling a joke are much funnier than others. On the other hand, if you change a key word, the joke may not make sense, or will lose its punch. Explaining too much in the beginning of a joke can give away the punch line in advance. Explaining too little can cause confusion.

What is the best timing for the joke?

Some people make a very long story out of a joke that could be told in a few short sentences. There is danger in making a joke extra long: Listening to the build-up* of a joke is work and it makes the listener anticipate a reward. The longer he or she listens, the better the punch line has to be.

If the joke is too short, there will be no tension built up for the punch line to release. If you thought the joke was funny the way you heard it, tell it using about the same amount of time.

There is usually a .pause* between the build-up of the joke and the punch line. This pause may be just a fraction of a second, but it can be very important to the listener's "getting" the joke. It gives the listener the time to understand all of the build-up. If the punch line comes too fast, the listener may still be digesting the previous information. Don't rush.

The rhythm of your speech, and the emphasis on certain words in the joke are important, too. Listen to joke tellers and practice imitating their rhythm. TV variety shows often have a **"stand-up comedian*"** telling jokes on a particular theme. Study their timing and their delivery. In some cities you can use your telephone to hear well-known comedians tell jokes. This is called Dial-a-Joke. You can look up the number for this service in the white pages of the telephone book. Or call Information for the number.

How's my pronunciation?

Poor pronunciation can kill a joke. Every word in a joke is important. If you are often asked to repeat your words in ordinary conversation, you may not be ready to tell jokes to a group of people. Practice on patient friends. Make a tape recording of some jokes and ask a friend to comment on where you are having difficulties. Drill the sounds that are a problem for you in English.

What can go wrong?

If you have paid attention to all of the tips above, you will have a greater rate of success. But there are still some times no one laughs at a joke. There may not be anything wrong with the joke, or with the way you told it. The listener may have heard the joke before, or it just doesn't strike her or him funny. (You win some, and you lose some.)

Do's and Don'ts

Do be sure you have your audience's attention, and that they are ready to listen. Speak clearly and energetically.

Don't introduce the joke as a joke. You can introduce it as a story, or say, "Did you hear the story about...." (And if they did hear it, DON'T TELL IT!)

Don't say, "This is a really funny joke," or "This one will really make you laugh." The appreciation of a joke is up to the listener.

Don't apologize for your joke either. Don't say, "This isn't really very funny," or "You've probably heard this one already."

Don't give away your punch line while you are introducing your joke.

Don't laugh while you are telling your joke.

Do be a good listener for the other person's joke. If someone tells a joke and you have heard that same joke told a little bit differently, don't tell it over your way. It won't be funny the second time and is rude to the teller of the first joke.

ANSWERS TO EXERCISES

CHAPTER ONE

I) 1. B;   2. A;   3. F;   4. I;   5. M;   6. D;
7. J;   8. E;   9. H;   10. K;   11. L;   12. C;
13. G.

II) 1. True;   2. False;   3. True;   4. True;   5. True;
6. False;   7. True;   8. True;   9. False;   10. False.

CHAPTER TWO

1. point;   2. butt;   3. authority;   4. punch line;
5. inferior;   6. stingy;   7. greedy;   8. deceitful;
9. hostility;   10. pause.

CHAPTER THREE

1. E;   2. C;   3. D;   4. H;   5. B;   6. G;
7. F;   8. A.

II) 1. 6;   2. A;   3. A;

CHAPTER FOUR

I) 1. J;   2. F;   3. A;   4. I;   5. B;   6. C;
7. G;   8. D;   9. E;   10. H;   11. K.

II) 1. a good catch;   2. get rid of;   3. show up;   4. in the
wrong;   5. strike back.

CHAPTER FIVE

I) 1. shatter;   2. passive;   3. munch;   4. complex;
5. mood;   6. vain.

II) 1. H;   2. G;   3. A;   4. J;   5. B;
6. C;   7. F;   8. K;   9. I;   10. D;   11. E;
12. N;   13. M.

CHAPTER SIX

1. caricature;   2. anecdotes;   3. brag;   4. custody.

CHAPTER SEVEN

1. butter up;   2. flunk;   3. grind;   4. foot the bills;
5. term paper;   6. toss a coin;   7. take back;
8. quarters;   9. pompous;   10. ambitious;   11. campus.

CHAPTER EIGHT

I) 1. E;   2. A;   3. L;   4. B;   5. C;
6. H;   7. I;   8. K;   9. G;   10. J;

11. F;   12. D.

II) 1. nun;   2. rabbi;   3. priest;   4. Pearly Gates;
    5. Saint Peter; 6. rosary beads;   7. services;
    8. blasphemy; 9. Sabbath;   10. chapel.

CHAPTER NINE
    1. specialist;   2. bedside manner;   3. diagnosis;
    4. cast;   5. recovery;   6. irrational;
    7. psychotherapist;   8. surgery;   9. consult.

CHAPTER TEN
I) 1. F;   2. A;   3. G;   4. C;   5. D;   6. E;
   7. H;   8. B.

CHAPTER ELEVEN
I) 1. discount;   2. crop;   3. parking meter;   4. turn-
      stile;   5. unreliable;   6. clumsy;   7. shortcut.

II) 1. E;   2. G;   3. B;   4. D;   5. C;   6. A;
    7. F;   8. H.

CHAPTER TWELVE
    1. head;   2. ripe;   3. thermos;   4. deli;   5. full
    bloom;   6. plantations;   7. light.

CHAPTER THIRTEEN
    1. enrich;   2. trespass;   3. malice;   4. luxury;
    5. offensive 6. barefoot;   7. Anglo-Saxon;   8. ethnic
    group;   9. mugger

CHAPTER FOURTEEN
    1. J;   2. I;   3. A;   4. B;   5. G;   6. C;
    7. D;   8. E;   9. F;   10. H.

CHAPTER FIFTEEN
    1. masochist,   sadist;   2. labor-saving devices;
    3. hire;   4. fire;   5. raise;   6. lizard;
    7. leisure;   8. somersaults;   9. cliff;
   10. go around   11. lottery;   12. site.

G L O S S A R Y

The definitions given here are solely for
the purpose of helping you understand the words
as they are used in this book; they are not
intended as complete definitions. If you wish
more information on these words or their correct
pronunciation, please use a standard dictionary.

absent-minded adj. Being unable to pay complete attention to what one
is doing because one's mind is busy thinking about romance, studies,
worries or other matters. "Betty was so absent-minded that she
never remembered where she had put her glasses."

abuse v. 1. To harm; treat cruelly. "Some unfortunate children are
continually abused by their parents." 2. To use for wrong pur
poses.
To use alcohol or drugs without sensible limits or self-control.

accident-prone adj. Having a tendency to have frequent accidents.
"Jack is the most accident-prone person I know. He's been in the
hospital seven times in the past three years."

acid rain n. Rain, made acid from air pollution from factory smoke.
It is very bad for farm and garden crops.

adjust v. Change or adapt to fit new conditions. "It takes time to
adjust to a new culture and make new friends."

aggression n. Bold or angry behavior.

ain't v. Uneducated general purpose negative. Non-standard. "I ain't
going." "Jack ain't no friend of mine." "We ain't ready." "They
ain't finished their work." Standard English in the previous
phrases would be **am not, isn't, aren't,** and **haven't**

alert adj. Wide awake, observant, intelligent. "Sue's baby is
so cute--and so alert at only three months." v. Warn, make
aware of some danger. "There are signs along the road to alert
drivers to sharp curves, hidden driveways, and deer crossings."

ambiguous adj. Words or situations that have two different meanings
or interpretations.

ambitious adj. Eager to work, willing to work hard in order to gain
a reward or goal. "An ambitious person can rise to the top position
in a small company."

ambulance n. A van to transport sick or injured people to the hospital.

anecdote n. A very short story.

Anglo-Saxon adj., n. Coming from England or Northern Germany.

anxiety n. Nervousness, stress, uneasiness, worry.

anxiety-provoking adj. Causing anxiety. "Violence on certain TV shows
can be anxiety-provoking for many children. "The news broadcast is
anxiety-provoking for most adults."

artificial adj. Not natural. Made in a laboratory. Imitation, not the real thing. "Many foods contain artificial coloring and flavoring." "Doctor's have given patients artificial hearts and artificial kidneys."

attractive adj. Good-looking. "This is an attractive package." "Jack and Helen are very attractive people."

auction n. A public sale at which things are sold to the person who bids the highest price.

authority n. Power, law, rule. "Parents have authority over their children."

background n. Family origin. "Bob has American Indian blood in his background." "Freda was ashamed of her background. She did not want anyone to know her parents were poor."

bacteria n. pl. Germs. One-celled organisms that can cause disease.

bald adj. Having no hair.

barefoot adj. Not wearing shoes or socks.

barnyard n. The yard or space around a barn (a building for farm animals).

barroom n. A place where one may buy beer, whiskey, or other alcoholic drinks at a bar.

bartender n. The person who works behind a bar, mixing and serving alcoholic drinks.

bedside manner n. The personality and caring attitude that a doctor shows his patients. "A doctor with a good bedside manner makes his patients feel confident in his judgement."

behalf; in behalf of, on behalf of In the interest of, for the benefit of; as an agent for. "On behalf of the people of my country, I would like to welcome you to the United States."

bigamy n. Marriage to two wives or two husbands. "Bigamy is illegal in the United States." A **bigamist** is a person who marries a second person without divorcing the first husband or wife.

bigot n. A prejudiced person who is full of hate for people of other races, nationalities or religions.

blaspheme v. Say words that are forbidden by the church.

blond, blonde adj. Having light-colored hair. n. a yellow-haired person.

bloom n. Flower. **in bloom** adj. Flowering. "The cherry trees will be in full bloom in late April." (full = at the highest point)

bolt of lightning n. A flash of lightning.

brag v. Boast. To talk about one's own superior qualities or possessions. "Ron bragged that he could beat anyone in a race."

bride n. A new wife. A woman who is getting married, or has just gotten married.

bruise v. To hurt the skin without breaking or cutting it. n. An injury to the skin.

build-up n. The beginning of a joke, that prepares the listener for the punch line.

bureaucrat n. A person who works at a government job.

burst into laughter v. Suddenly start to laugh noisily.

butt n. The object of a joke. The person or group of people that is made fun of in a joke.

butter up v. Flatter (give false compliments) for the purpose of gaining some advantage.

campus n. At a college, the area that includes the school buildings, student dormitories, and recreation areas.

candidate n. A person who wishes to be elected to a position such as president, senator, governor, congressman, mayor, etc.

canvas n. The tightly stretched heavy cloth on which an artist paints.

carefree adj. Having no problems or worries. "It's great to be young, single, and carefree."

caricature n. A picture that **exaggerates*** the characteristics of the subject.

cast n. The hard plaster or metal support for a broken arm or leg. "Jim had his leg in a cast for six weeks after the accident."

catch, good catch n. slang. A person with money, a good job, good looks, high status or power, who would be a good person to marry.

cave n. A large opening in the side of a hill or mountain, which can serve as a home for an animal. **Cavemen** n. Early humans who lived in caves many thousands of years ago.

cemetery n. A graveyard. A place where dead bodies are buried.

challenge v. Call to engage in a fight or contest. "Joe challenged Pete to a race." n. "The job of a police officer offers many challenges to a bright young man or woman."

chubby adj. Fat, in a pleasing, babylike way.

chuckle v. To laugh softly. n. Soft, gentle laughter.

circulation n. The movement of the blood from the heart through the arteries and veins and back to the heart.

cliff n. A completely verticle side of a hill or mountain.

clumsy adj. Awkward. Having no skill or coordination. "A clumsy person falls easily or drops and breaks things easily."

coach n. A person who teaches athletes how to perform certain sports.

131

cockroach n. A flat-bodied insect that lives in the cracks of the walls in people's homes, particularly in large apartment buildings.

coffee-to-go n. Coffee served in a covered plastic cup so it may be taken out of the store or restaurant.

combat v. Fight. "The hardest things we have to combat are poverty and ignorance."

comes in threes v. To occur in a set of three. "Some people believe that bad luck always comes in threes."

complex adj. Complicated. Having many parts. Difficult to understand. "Reasons for the high divorce rate in America are very complex."

conflict n. A Disagreement, battle or war.

consult v. See someone to get advice or information. "Have you ever consulted a fortune teller?"

contract v. Make or become smaller. "Air contracts as it cools, and expands as it becomes warmer.

convention n. A formal meeting of members or representatives of an organized group such as a political party, or a professional group such as teachers.

convulsive adj. Shaking violently.

cope v. Deal with. Handle a problem or a situation successfully. "A fireman copes with danger every day." "Mrs. J. had a hard time **coping** with her twin boys—they were always into trouble."

corruption n. Dishonesty, as in government. Using an elected position to gain extra profits, take illegal payments for favors, etc.

counselor n. A person who gives advice to help another. "Mr. and Mrs. Z. are going to a marriage counselor to help them solve their difficulties."

crab n. 1. A shellfish. 2. An unpleasant, complaining person. v. To complain constantly. **crabby** adj.

cram v. To study for hours just before a test.

criminal 1. n. A person who breaks the law—a thief, robber, murderer, etc. 2. adj. Referring to crime or its punishment.

crisis n. Emergency. Critical situation. The moment of greatest danger in a story, an illness or an international situation.

criticize v. To judge the good and bad points of a person or thing. To tell the faults or bad points.

crop n. Farm products such as fruit, vegetables, or **grains***.

crook n. A criminal. A dishonest person, such as a liar, a thief or a cheater.

crutches n. Devices used to help a person walk. "Larry walked on crutches for a month while his ankle was healing."

132

cupboard n. A small closet in kitchen for dishes, canned food, or other objects.

curse 1. v. To call on God to bring bad luck or punishment to someone or something. To say vulgar words. "Paul got so angry, he cursed for five minutes straight." 2. n. Vulgar words. "Dan thought it was funny to teach his two-year-old child a few curses to shock the neighbors with."

custody n. The right granted by a court to a parent to be the guardian of a child or children. The child lives with the parent who has custody. "Mr. and Mrs. Black got divorced; he got custody of the older boy, and she got custody of the two young girls."

darn it interjection. A euphemism for the more vulgar "damn it!" An expression of anger.

deaf adj. Unable to hear.

dean n. The person at a school who advises students and enforces rules about student behavior.

debate v. Discuss opposite sides of an issue. n. A formal discussion.

deceitful adj. Lying. Not to be trusted.

degree n. Extent. A comparative intensity or quality of something. "Mary was content with her job to a certain degree, but she often thought that she could be earning more money."

deli n. Delicatessen. A small grocery store in which one may buy food-to-go, such as sandwiches, salads, coffee, buttered rolls, etc.

deliver the punch line see **punchline**.

depressed adj. Sad.

derogatory adj. Having an attitude of contempt, hatred, or disgust for a person or group of people. "Stella made several derogatory comments about her neighbors."

deserted adj. Empty. Having no people. "The streets were deserted at eleven p.m."

diagnose v. To examine and form an opinion about the cause of a sickness. **diagnosis** n. the doctor's opinion about a person's sickness.

discount n. A reduction or lowering of the price for something.

dominant adj. Most important. Being in control or having the most influence.

dominating adj. Controlling by means of superior power.

dope n. A stupid person.

dormitory n. A room or building used for sleeping quarters for a number of people such as students at a college.

double talk n. Speech that is hard to understand because it is deliberately complex, with long, many-syllabled words, and difficult structure. "Sarah wished her lawyer would stop talking double-talk, and speak plain English so she could understand him."

drive n. Energy used to accomplish a task or achieve satisfaction. An inner motivation or need to pursue some goal such as sex, power, status, wealth, freedom, excellence, etc. "To become president of an organization, a person needs intelligence, ability and a strong drive."

dumb 1. adj. Stupid. "You dumb ox!" she screamed. "I told you not to open the door." 2. adj. Unable to speak; mute. "Gary was struck dumb when he saw that his car had been towed away."

dummy n. A stupid person.

dump v. Throw away, as garbage and trash. n. The place where garbage is brought by the garbage trucks. (slang) A place or building that is very poor, ugly, old, and dirty.

dull adj. 1. Boring. 2. Not very intelligent.

earthquake n. Violent movement of the earth.

ease n. Easiness. An absence of difficulty. "She repaired the motor with ease, which surprised all the men." v. To make easier, to smooth out the rough parts. Remove tensions from a situation. "Mrs. B. was worried about her sick child, but a phone call to the doctor eased her mind."

economy n. The money situation of a family or a government. "The economy of Saudi Arabia is based largely on oil."

economic recession see recession.

edible. adj. Good to eat. "The flowers of some plants are edible, if you know how to cook them properly."

e.g. For example.

endorphin n. A natural chemical produced by the brain. It acts to reduce anxiety and stop pain.

enforce v. Make or compel people to obey a law. "The job of the police is to enforce the law." "It is easy to make a law against smoking marijuana, but it is very difficult to enforce that law."

enrich v. Make richer or better in some way. "The study of literature will enrich your life."

epidemic n. The rapid spread of a contagious disease. "Last winter there was an epidemic of flu."

ethnic group n. A group of people with a common culture or language, such as American Blacks, Puerto Ricans, Polish, Germans, Irish, etc.

ethnic background n. The language and nationality of one's parents and grandparents. "What's Carl's ethnic background?" "He's part Irish, part German and part Italian."

evict v. Force a tenant to move out of a rented apartment or house. "The landlord evicted the Smiths for not paying their rent."

exaggerate v. Increase or enlarge a fact. "Aggie always exaggerates. If she feels a drop of rain, and a little wind, she says it's a terrible rainstorm."

expectant adj. Expecting a baby. Pregnant. "The hospital has classes in child care for expectant mothers."

expense, laugh at someone's expense To make another person the butt of a joke. "The whole office laughed at the boss's expense.

expert n. A person with great knowledge in a particular field.

extermination n. Complete destruction; killing all of a certain life form. "The people wished to exterminate the rats in their town."

formerly adv. Before. Previously. "Mrs. Ronald White was previously known as Jane Jones."

fad n. A style of clothing, game, or joke that is temporarily popular with many people.

fall through. v. Fail to be completed. Be unsuccessful. "X Company planned to buy a building in New York, but the deal fell through."

federal adj. Having to do with the national government. "Each year on April 15th, Americans file their federal income tax reports."

fee n. The price for a service. "The lawyer's fee was $100."

filter v. Take out the dirt or impurities in a liquid by straining it through cloth or paper.

fire v. Dismiss or discharge an employee from his or her job. "The boss fired Dan because he always arrived late to work."

fit adj. Suitable. Good enough for someone or some purpose. "This is a dinner fit for a king."

flatter v. Compliment in order to win some favor, or to please a person. "You have beautiful eyes," he said. "Stop flattering me," she said. "I'm not flattering you, I really mean it," he replied.

flattering adj. Causing to appear in a favorable light. "That's not a very flattering dress Sue is wearing."

flexible adj. Capable of being bent or changed. "Flexible people can adapt to new situations easily."

flock n. Group of animals or birds, such as a flock of sheep or a flock of chickens.

fluent adj. Capable of speaking a language at normal conversational speed. "Janet is fluent in Spanish, French, and Japanese."

flunk v. Fail a test or course of subject at school.

folklore n. The collection of stories, legends, and fairy tales told by the people of a country.

foot the bills v. (slang) Pay the expenses.

fractured adj. or v. past tense. Broken. (said of bones)

fraternity n. A social group of boys or men who have some common interest or purpose.

fraternity house n. A building at a college or school where members of a fraternity live.

frustrated adj. v. past tense. Annoyed, disappointed and discouraged by not being able to accomplish one's purpose. "Mary was frustrated when she was late and her car would not start."

fuel n. Something that is burned in order to produce heat or power. "Gas, oil, and wood are fuels."

full bloom, in n. see **bloom**.

funeral n. The ceremony conducted before burying a dead person. "Mr. Clark died yesterday morning. The funeral will be held at two p.m. tomorrow afternoon, at the Friendly Funeral Home."

fussy adj. Particular. Hard-to-please. "Many children are fussy eaters." "Betty is very fussy about who she gives her telephone number to."

gee whiz interjection. A mild exclamation of surprise or annoyance.

generate v. Cause to begin or grow. Produce. "The attempted assassination of the President generated a lot of sympathy for him." "**Fuel*** is burned to generate electrical power."

generous adj. Giving willingly. Kind.

get v. Understand. "Mac didn't get the joke."

get away with murder Murder (kill) someone and not be punished.

get rid of v. Remove something that is harmful or annoying. "We used poison to get rid of the mice in our house."

give a break v. Give an opportunity to do something. Remove a difficulty or a barrier.

give up v. Surrender. Stop trying to accomplish something. "Dick tried to solve the problem, but he had to give up."

go around v. Be enough for everybody. "There was enough lemonade to go around."

go up v. Increase in price or value.

go over one's head To be impossible to understand. "The professor's speech went over my head."

goodie goodie n. A person who is overly good or well-behaved. This kind of person makes other people feel uncomfortable.

got a light? Do you have a match I can light my cigarette with?

graffiti n. plural. Pictures or writings written so they may be seen by the public, such as on walls in buses, trains, or public bathrooms.

grain n. A farm crop such as rice, oats, barley, wheat, and corn.

Grand Canyon n. A mile-high canyon carved out by the Colorado River. Located in the state of Arizona, it is a major tourist attraction in the United States.

grandfather clock n. An old-fashioned clock that works by a pendulum. It is usually in a cabinet as tall as a person.

grave n. The place (usually a hole in the ground) where a dead body is buried.

greasy spoon n. A cheap, inferior restaurant. The food is not good and the dishes are not always perfectly clean.

greedy adj. Selfish. Wanting to have a very large quantity of food, money, goods for oneself, without considering other people's needs.

grind n. (slang) Boring, difficult work that must be done every day. "Hal's vacation was over, so now it was back to the old grind."

grumpy adj. Bad-tempered. Easily made angry. Irritable. "Father is always grumpy when he has to wait for his dinner."

grunt n. The sound a pig makes. v. To make a sound like a pig in disgust or annoyance. "Mr. Brown looked up from his newspaper and grunted hello to us as we walked in."

guilt n. Responsibility for doing something wrong. A bad feeling that comes from having hurt another person.

hand over v. Give possession of something to someone else. "As soon as Bob received the payment for the car, he handed over the keys."

handicap n. A disability, such as blindness, deafness, or inability to speak, walk or perform necessary functions normally.

hard-of-hearing adj. Deaf. Unable to hear well.

harp n. A stringed musical instrument. In Christian mythology, angels play beautiful music in Heaven on their harps.

have it easy Have an easy time or an easy life. "Compared to Japanese students, American school children have it easy—classes five hours a day, just five days a week, with not very much homework."

have one's eyes opened Become aware of facts that were previously hidden.

have the nerve Have courage. Dare. Do something bold or socially difficult. "Pat never has the nerve to stand up and say what she thinks."

headquarters n. plural The central location or office of a military force or a police force.

head (of a nail) n. The flat part that is hit by the hammer.

heads and tails on a coin All American coins have the picture of a famous American on one side and a symbol such as an eagle, a famous building, the Liberty Bell etc. on the other side. "Heads" refers to the side with the head. "Tails" is the other side.

health food   n.   Food that is especially grown, free from chemical additives, poisons, bug-killers, artificial colorings or preservatives.

health food store   A special store where health food and vitamins are sold.

hire   v.   Take on a new employee at a job.   "Mr. Grant will hire two new secretaries this week."

hobby   n.   An interest or activity a person does for enjoyment, such as collecting coins or stamps, gardening, reading.

honk   n.   The sound of a car's horn.

hormone   n.   A chemical product of a gland in the body that travels through the blood causing or allowing some other organs to function or change.

house call   n.   A visit by a doctor to the home of a sick patient.

hostility   n.   Angry and aggressive feelings or behavior.

hurdle   n.   Barrier. Obstacle. Something that one must jump over in order to continue running in the same path.

idiom   n.   A vocabulary item that consists of more than a single word.

ignorant   adj.   1. Not knowing about something. "George was ignorant of the facts in the matter." 2. Uneducated, stupid. "Pete is an ignorant person."

i.e.   "Id est." A latin abbreviation = that is. In other words.

illogic   n.   Not logic. Behavior that is not based on reason.

illustrate   v.   Draw pictures for a book or a story.

imply   v.   Suggest or hint at something without actually saying it. "Bob's behavior towards Alice implies that he is no longer in love with her."

inability   n.   Lack of ability. Powerlessness in a certain area. "Bob's inability to type caused him to lose his job."

in the wrong   Wrong. On the wrong side of an argument or discussion. Being the cause of a problem. "Jennie apologized when she realized she had been in the wrong."

incompetent   adj.   Unskilled. Unable to do one's job or a task.

indigestion   n.   An upset stomach. Nausea. A stomach ache from eating too much, or eating food that is difficult to digest.

inferior   adj.   Lower in quality or status. "Sometimes a cheaper price just means you are buying inferior goods." "Ted felt inferior to his classmates, because he was poor."

inflation n. A continuous rise in prices and wages. "The high cost of oil was one of the causes of inflation."

influence v. Act in a way that will cause another person to change his character, behavior, or thought.

ingratitude n. Lack of appreciation. "Don gave his children everything, but received nothing but ingratitude in return."

inherited adj. Gotten from one's parents or relatives. "Gene inherited his mother's blue eyes." 2. "Charles inherited a fortune when his uncle died."

in line Behaving properly, according to social standards. "Mrs. Clark keeps her six kids in line by frequent spankings."

inmate n. A person who lives in an institution such as a mental hospital or a prison.

insane adj. Crazy. Not sane.

insecure adj. Not safe. "Janet felt insecure living all by herself so she bought a large dog for protection."

instinct n. Behavior that is inborn, and does not have to be learned. "A mother cat takes care of her babies by instinct."

interaction n. Action (conversation, business deals, romance, fights, etc.) between two people or groups.

interfere v. Make it difficult for another person to do what he or she is doing. "The sounds of the neighbor's TV interfered with Tom's doing his homework."

interpret v. To make someone's meaning clear. To translate.

intrigue v. To cause someone to be interested or curious about something. "The title of the book intrigued her, so she bought it."

irrational adj. Not rational. Not reasonable. Illogical. "Ken was so angry he became completely irrational and started throwing furniture around the room."

irrationality n. Nonsense. Lack of reasoning power.

irritate v. Annoy. Disturb. "The constant buzzing of flies around her head irritated her."

jolly adj. Happy, cheerful.

key word n. A word necessary to the understanding of a subject. An essential or important word in the story.

kid v. Tease. Make gentle fun at someone's expense. "Mark's friends all kidded him about his beautiful long hair."

knock someone out v. Hit someone so hard that he or she becomes unconscious. "The robber knocked his victim out before taking his money."

labor-saving devices n. Machines or tools that save work. "The vacuum cleaner is a labor-saving device."

lack n. Absence of something; the state of not having. "The farmers are worried about their corn crop because of the lack of rain."
v. Needing but not having something. "Walter has money and good looks, but he lacks brains."

leash n. A rope or chain to hold a pet such as a dog or a cat.

leisure n. Free time. Time after working hours.

liberated adj. (slang) Free from traditional ideas of the status and roles of men and women. "A liberated male is not afraid to wash dishes."

living n. earn a **living**. Work for the money one needs to pay for rent, food, clothing, etc.

lizard n. A reptile that looks like a small alligator. A cold-blooded, four-legged animal, covered with scales.

lobster n. A seafood specialty. A shellfish that has large claws.

long-winded adj. Capable of talking for a very long time.

lose one's **mind** v. Become insane. Go crazy.

lottery n. A contest to win money by chance. Tickets are sold to raise money, then numbers are drawn. The people who have tickets with the same numbers win the prizes. "Frank won a thousand dollars in the lottery."

lowest-ranking adj. see **rank**.

lousy adj. (slang) Bad, miserable, worthless. Of very poor quality. "The weather was lousy."

lungs n. The organs used for breathing.

lump together v. Group together in the same category as if they were the same thing. "Many New Yorkers lump all Spanish-speakers together as Puerto Ricans."

luxury n. Wealth. Richness.

magnify v. Make larger.

malice n. A desire to hurt other people.

malign v. Do harm to. Speak about in a hurtful way.

manipulate v. To control or influence. **manipulative** adj. Controlling the behavior of others for one's own selfish interest.

manure n. Droppings of farm animals used as fertilizer.

martini n. An alcoholic drink.

masochist n. A person who enjoys receiving pain.

material n. Anything that is used to make something else. "Wood is a good material to build a house with." 2. Related to the enjoyment of physical comfort or health. "Bea did not want material things such as a new car or fancy clothes; she wanted the love of

140

a good man."

maximum n. The greatest possible amount or number.

measles n. A sickness that causes a fever, a sore throat, and red, itchy spots on the skin.

meddlesome adj. Entering into other people's personal business.

Miami n. A large city in the state of Florida. A tourist resort famous for sandy beaches and night clubs.

minimize v. Make smaller.

minister n. The religious leader of a church.

minority n. Opposite of majority. Fewer than half of the group. "The majority of congressmen this year are Republicans; the minority are Democrats."

moan v. To cry softly in pain. n. A low cry of sadness or pain."

mock v. To make fun of. To ridicule by exaggerated imitation. "Tom hated it when his wife mocked him in front of other people."

modify v. Change some of the features of. "Over the years, wind and rain have modified the shape of the hill."

monogamy n. Marriage to one husband or one wife.

mood n. A state of feeling. "Getting a raise in pay put Sam in an excellent mood." "Don't bother Daddy now, he's in a bad mood."

mud pack n. A treatment done in a beauty parlor to clean and freshen the skin. Special mud is spread on the face, kept on for a short time, and then cleaned off.

mugger n. A robber who attacks and robs people in the street.

mule n. A large, strong, but sometimes stubborn work animal, the offspring of a horse and a donkey.

munch v. Chew noisily.

nag v. Complain, scold, and continually find things to criticize. Repeatedly urge someone to do something they have no desire to do. "Don't nag me to take out the garbage--I'll do it when I finish the newspaper."

neurological adj. Having to do with the nervous system.

neurotic n. A person suffering from a disorder of the mind or emotion that results in anxiety, phobias or inappropriate behavior.

nick-name n. A shortened form of a formal name. A descriptive informal name. "Bob is a nick-name for Robert." "Paul's nick-name was Lefty, because he was left-handed."

notorious adj. Famous, but for negative reasons.

nuclear reactor n. An atomic pile. A device that produces heat to generate electrical power, using nuclear energy from uranium and other radioactive elements.

nun n. A woman who belongs to a special group of women who spend their lives working for the church, praying, teaching, and doing good work in the name of the church.

nutty adj. (slang) Slightly insane.

obscene adj. Referring to words, pictures or behavior that are considered indecent and offensive.

obstacle n. Something or some one who stands in the way of progress towards a goal. A barrier or hindrance.

odor n. Fragrance, smell. "A skunk has a bad odor."

offensive adj. Causing anger; disagreeable to the senses. "Joe's statements about Jews were offensive to Larry."

omnipotent adj. All-powerful. Capable of doing anything. "God is supposed to be omnipotent."

opponent n. Enemy. The opposite side in a contest or battle.

oppose v. To be on the opposite side in an argument or battle. To be against something. "Many people opposed the new law."

ornery adj. Stubborn, nasty, or having an unpleasant personality.

out of tune adj. Not musically perfect. "The piano was out of tune, so Miss Clark called the piano tuner."

overwhelm v. Overpower, defeat; knock over with excess physical or emotional force. "Eva's perfume overwhelmed me when I walked in."

pace v. Walk with evenly-measured steps. "The lion paced back and forth in his small cage."

palm n. The inner side of the hand.

paradox n. A statement that seems contradictory or impossible, yet is true.

parking meter n. Coins are put into this to pay for the right to park a car for a certain period of time.

party in power n. The political party of the president and the majority of the law-making branch of government.

passive adj. Meek, quiet, unable to begin an action alone. A passive person may be follower, and accept orders without complaining or objecting.

pasture n. A grassy area where cows and horses may feed.

pause v. Stop for a short time before continuing. "The speaker paused for a moment to check his notes." n. A brief rest.

peck v. Hit with the beak. (A bird's hard mouth is called a beak.)

pecking order n. A system among chickens, ducks, etc., wherein

142

the strongest individual may peck at all others; the second
strongest allows himself to be pecked by the strongest, but
he pecks all the weaker ones, and so on down the line. The
weakest member of the flock is pecked by all the others.

pesticide n. A chemical poison used to kill insects or rats.

phooey interjection. An expression of extreme disgust. "Phooey!
This food tastes rotten!"

play on words Using words with double meanings, or words that sound
similar to other words to create humor.

plantation n. A very large farm (in the South) on which cotton,
tobacco, coffee, or similar crops are grown.

poke fun at v. Make fun of. Ridicule. Tease. "It's not nice to
poke fun at fat people."

point of a joke The reason a joke is funny. "I don't get it. What's
the point?"

pollution n. Dirt or poisons in the air or water.

pompous adj. Arrogant, self-important. Behaving or talking in a way
that shows that one feels superior to and more important than
others. "The new mayor is a pompous fool, in my opinion."

Pop n. Familiar word for father. Dad.

poverty n. The state of being poor. "Abraham Lincoln was born into
poverty, but he became President of the United States."

preoccupied adj. Worried, concerned. "Dad was preoccupied with
business problems all evening, so he didn't talk much."

prejudice adj. Judging before having all the facts. A feeling that
a person of another race or nationality is inferior, dirty,
unreliable or dangerous because of his race or nationality.

preservative n. A substance used to prolong the life or the
freshness of food.

privilege n. A special permission or benefit given to someone because
he or she is older, richer, in a position of power or of a
certain social class. "For punishment, Mother took Roberto's
privileges away. Now he can't watch TV, use the family car, or
stay out after eleven p.m."

prize v. To value highly. To be proud of. "Kraisorn prizes his
American citizenship." "New Yorkers prize their museums and
theaters, but there is no sign that they prize clean streets."

provoke v. To make angry, to annoy. To cause someone to fight. "If
you keep talking that way, you might provoke a fight."

psychiatrist n. A medical doctor who is licensed to treat mental
illness.

psychoanalyst n. A psychiatrist who uses the analytical methods of
Sigmund Freud in treating neurosis.

psychologist n. A person trained to do psychological research,

143

therapy, or analysis. This usually requires a Ph.D. but the person is not a medical doctor.

psychotherapist n. A person who treats people who have mental, emotional or behavioral problems. This is the most common and general word, usually shortened to "therapist," or more casually, "head-shrink." (One who "shrinks heads," a slang term that comes from the custom of certain primitive tribes in Brazil who shrink their enemies' heads after they have killed them, and wear the shrunken heads on their belts.)

psychotic adj. Insane, crazy. n. A person who is insane, completely out of contact with reality.

punch line n. The last sentence or words of a joke that make people laugh. **deliver the punch line** To say the punch line. "The comedian paused before delivering the punch line."

pun n. A short joke that depends on word play. (Using different senses of the same word, or twisting the pronunciation of a word so that it sounds like another.)

punctual adj. On time. Never late.

push around v. Dominate by means of superior strength or power. "Hank got tired of being pushed around by his big brother."

putt-putting v. Making a sound of a bubbly little motor.

puzzle n. A game, toy, or problem that must be solved, assembled, or explained. v. Confuse. "Jack's behavior puzzled Ann."

quarters n. pl. A place to live. A building or section of a building in which people live. "Joe's living quarters were small, but comfortable."

rabbi n. The leader of a Jewish congregation (group of people who attend the same synagogue or temple).

ragged adj. Torn, worn-out. Full of holes.

raise n. An increase in pay.

ranch n. A large farm on which animals (horses, cattle, sheep, etc.) are raised.

rank n. Station, status, or class. A position in society or military force. "General is a higher rank than sergeant." **lowest-ranking** adj. Being at the bottom of the social ladder.

recession n. A temporary period of economic slowness, with unemployment and poor business activity. A recession that lasts for a long time is a **depression.**

recommend v. Advise. Tell about the good qualities of a person, place or thing. "Can you recommend a good place to eat?"

recover v. Become well after an illness. **recovery** n. The act of getting well after an illness. "Larry made a quick recovery from his cold."

red tape n. Legal and governmental application papers and forms which must be filled out when dealing with government agencies.

"You have to go through a lot of red tape if you want to change your name on your social security card."

reduce v. Make smaller. Lose weight. Lower the price of something for sale.

reflex n. A natural and unlearned reaction to an action or a condition.

refrain (from) v. To prevent oneself from doing something. To hold oneself back; restrain oneself. "Please refrain from smoking."

reinforce v. Add strength to. To add extra support, or increase the number of something.

relieve v. To lesson something that is painful; take away pain, fear, tension, anxiety, or give someone a rest from doing a difficult job. "Put ice on your forehead to relieve a headache."

relief n. Anything that takes away or lessens pain, fear, tension, anxiety, hard work, etc.

researcher n. A person who thoroughly studies some area of knowledge.

resent v. Be angry (and possibly jealous) because of another person's actions, or superior powers, possessions, or rewards. "Al resented all the special favors his younger brothers got, while he worked just as hard and got nothing."

resentment n. Anger felt as a result of some action of others or as a result of unfair treatment.

reserve v. Keep or save for later; save for a special purpose or for a special person.

restore v. Bring back. Place something in the original place from which it was taken or from which it disappeared.

riddle n. A question that is difficult to answer and requires careful thought. It often has a surprise or an unexpected answer.

ridicule v. Make fun of. Say or do things that will make others laugh at a certain person, group of people, idea, or object.

ripe adj. Ready to be picked from the plant and used or eaten. "The apples aren't ripe, you'll get a stomach ache if you eat them."

risk v. To do something that might be dangerous. To disregard safety warnings. n. Possible danger.

rival n. Competitor. "Friendly" enemy, such as opposing teams from neighboring colleges. Someone who is trying to gain the same prize. "Carl was heart-broken. His girlfriend just married his rival."

rural adj. Not densely populated. An area of farms and forests.

Sabbath n. A day of rest and going to church. Sunday is the Sabbath for Christians, Saturday is the Sabbath for Jews.

saber-toothed tiger n. A kind of tiger with extremely long, powerful teeth. These tigers lived millions of years ago and are now extinct. (no longer living)

sacrifice v. To give up something of value for another purpose or to achieve a goal. "Should you sacrifice good quality to buy something at a cheaper price?" n. The thing given up. "Mr. Jones made many sacrifices so his children could get an education."

sadist n. A person who enjoys hurting other people.

safety valve n. A valve (opening) in an engine or a steam boiler that opens automatically when the pressure gets too high. 2. A way to allow explosive emotions escape harmlessly.

sail v. To move over water, as a ship does. 2. To fly as smoothly through the air as a ship goes through the water.

Saint Peter n. One of the followers of Jesus Christ. He is pictured as being the guardian of the gates to Heaven.

saloon n. A place where alcoholic drinks are served at a bar.

sanity n. Mental health. The opposite of craziness. "After working in that busy office for two months, Ralph thought he would lose his sanity."

sarcastic adj. Bitter humor. Humor that shows a strong feeling of antagonism, annoyance or controlled anger. Often the opposite of what is really meant is said. "A stranger accidentally stepped hard on Marcia's foot. "Don't worry about it", she said. "I've got another one." (foot. This one is broken now.)

say one's rosary v. A Catholic practice of repeating certain prayers, counting the number of prayers by moving a rosary bead on a string for each time the prayer is said.

scaffold n. A device that painters and other workmen stand on when they are painting or working on the side of a building. By pulling ropes, they can lower or raise themselves.

scandal n. Public knowledge of acts that are considered immoral or shocking. Public disgrace. Improper behavior by famous people or government officials that is well-publicized by gossip or by being printed in the newspapers. "Every year there is a new scandal about some member of Congress."

scold v. Speak to someone harshly in order to correct behavior or punish for misbehaving. **scolding** n. Harsh criticism given in anger. "Billy's mother gave him a scolding for breaking her vase."

sense of humor n. The ability to see the funny side of things, to appreciate and create jokes or witty comments.

sequence n. Order, from beginning to end.

shatter v. Break (as glass does) into little pieces.

shed blood v. Spill blood. Cut. Wound or injure intentionally.

shipwreck n. The destruction of a ship by a storm or by breaking against large rocks, or crashing into another ship. **shipwrecked sailor** A sailor who has survived the wreck of his ship, escaping in a life raft or by swimming to shore.

shortcomings n. Fault or failure in ability, performance, or personality. "Pete has his shortcomings—he drinks, he can't keep a job, he has a bad temper—but his wife loves him all the same." "Nobody is perfect; we all have our shortcomings."

shortcut n. A short way to go somewhere or do something.

show up v. Make an appearance. Come to some event such as a party, class, meeting. "Twenty people said they would come to the meeting, but only seven actually showed up."

sideline n. A job that one does in addition to one's regular job. In a store, a secondary item or group of items for sale, not as important or extensive as the main line. "My teacher plays in a band on weekends as a sideline."

Sistine Chapel A famous church in Rome, a part of Saint Peter's Cathedral. The ceiling of this chapel was painted by the famous artist Michelangelo.

site n. Location of a town or building. The ground on which a building is situated, or will be built.

skull n. The head bone. The protection for the brain.

sloppy adj. Messy. Not neat. "Shirley's room was always sloppy."

slur v. To speak carelessly, with poor pronunciation. A drunk person might slur when he speaks.

smooth over v. Remove the wrinkles from; to soothe, to make calm. To remove the tensions from some situation. "John called Mary to apologise for his rudeness. This helped smooth over the bad feelings between them."

So-and-So n. This expression is used when the name of a person is not known, or the speaker does not wish to mention it. "So-and-So told me that Milly and Jack were getting divorced."

soap opera n. An afternoon television story, in the form of a serial, with continuing action of the same characters each day. Most of the advertisements on these shows are by companies who make soap and cleaning supplies.

sober adj. Not drunk. Free from the effects of alcohol.

somersault n. Moving with one's head and knees tucked close to the chest.

snore v. Make a deep sound in the back of the throat or nose while sleeping.

specialist n. A person who knows a great deal about a particular field of knowledge. A doctor who works only on a certain part of the body.

split one's sides v. To laugh extremely hard, until it hurts.

spouse n. Husband or wife.

stagger v. Walk clumsily, unbalanced. Walk like a drunk person, almost falling with each step.

stand-up comedian n. A professional entertainer whose act consists of

147

telling jokes. **comedienne** (feminine form)

steep adj. Almost perpendicular. Having a sharp incline. "The house is on a steep hill."

stereotype n. A conventional and usually over-simplified (and certainly not always true!) idea of what a member of a certain group is like. Some examples: "College professors are very forgetful; Japanese people always carry cameras."

stew n. A meal of meat, potatoes and vegetables in a thick soup or gravy.

stickup n. A street robbery. "'Stick up your hands!' said the robber, as he pointed a gun at the two women."

stigma n. A sign of something that is socially unacceptable. A mark of disgrace. "There used to be a stigma attached to getting a divorce, but not any more."

still n. A device used for manufacturing alcohol from corn or other grain.

stimulate v. Cause the beginning of or the increase of an action. "Read a good book each week; it will stimulate your thinking."

stingy adj. Unwilling to spend money or give things to others.

stock broker n. A person who is licensed to sell stocks (shares of ownership in a large corporation).

straighten out v. Fix. Cure. End confusion by explanations.

strike back v. Hit the person who hit one first. "If you annoy Fred, he is likely to strike back in some way."

struggle v. To use a great deal of energy to deal with something.

sue v. To hire a lawyer and take a person to court in order to gain money owed or due to one because of harm or damages caused by the other person. "Victor sued the driver of the other car for fifty thousand dollars."

superior adj. Older or more important than. Having more authority or power. Of a higher social status or position. n. Any person in authority such as a parent, teacher, supervisor, or boss.

supervise v. To oversee and manage the work or behavior of others. **supervision** n. "Parents are responsible for the proper supervision of their children in public."

surgery n. Treating a diseased or injured condition of the body by operating with instruments to cut, repair, sew, or change a part of the body in some way. "Ken was shot by a robber, and had to have surgery to remove the bullet from his chest."

survive v. To continue to live in spite of a dangerous or difficult experience. "Seven people survived the plane crash."

taboo adj. Forbidden. n. Something that is forbidden. "It is taboo to speak about certain organs of the body in polite company."

take a shot v. Attempt to hit.

take back v. Apologize for having said something insulting. "I'm sorry, I take it back. I was wrong about you."

take for granted v. To consider a person or thing without suitable appreciation of its real value. To forget to give proper attention to. "Most of us take our health for granted until we become ill." "Sue wished her husband would not take her for granted."

take it out on v. To express anger, not necessarily on the proper person or object. "Don was angry at his boss, but he took it out on his girlfriend."

tarnished adj. Covered with a film of oxidized metal. "The silver is tarnished and needs to be polished."

tee n. 1. The starting mound from which a golf ball is hit. 2. A small device used to hold the golf ball above the ground.

tension n. Strain, such as that produced by the stretching a rubber band or pushing on a spring. Emotional strain.

term paper n. A written assignment in a college class that requires thought, research, and organization of ideas. One such major paper may be required for a term (semester) of a course.

thermos n. An insulated bottle for keeping liquids hot or cold. "Sy filled his thermos with hot coffee every morning."

thoroughly adv. Completely.

tickle v. Touch the body lightly. "She tickled the baby under the chin, causing him to laugh." **Tickling** n.

tickle one's funny bone v. Make someone laugh. Appear funny. "The cartoon tickled Harry's funny bone."

tie the knot v. (slang) Get married.

timid adj. Shy. Not brave.

tip n. A small bit of advice. Information that can help one become successful. "Professor Jones he gave his writing students many helpful tips for improving their stories."

tolerant adj. Having an easygoing personality. Able to permit many varied behaviors of others without forbidding them or reacting negatively. **tolerate** v. To permit or allow other people to hold their own beliefs, opinions and behaviors even though one does not agree with or approve of them.

tonic n. A food or medicine that increases the ability of the body to function.

toss a coin Throw a coin (a nickel, dime, etc.) up in the air to see which side will come down face up (see **heads or tails**). A decision may be made on the result.

tragedy n. Something very sad. A story with a sad ending.

traffic jam n. A slowing down or stopping of the movement of cars on a road. "There is a traffic jam on Route 4 every day at five p.m."

tremor n. Tremblings. Shaking. "Victor had muscle tremors with his high fever."

trespass v. To enter a private building or land without permission of the owner.

trial n. **on trial** To be judged in a court of law.

trigger n. The device on a gun (pressed by the finger) that causes the bullet to fire. v. To cause an event to happen.

try v. To judge in a court of law. "They tried the prisoner and found him guilty of murder."

turn down v. Refuse. Say no to a proposition. "Sam went to the bank and asked for a loan, but they turned him down."

turnstile n. A device at a public place that collects money from people who wish to enter. After one puts in the proper coin, the arm of the turnstile turns allowing one person to enter.

twist v. Turn, using pressure. n. An unexpected change or development. "O. Henry wrote many stories that ended with a twist."

umgawa This is a nonsense word. It was created to sound like Indian language, but has no actual meaning.

underlying adj. Supporting. Forming the foundation of something. Lying under.

unintelligible adj. Not easily understood. He spoke so softly he was completely unintelligible.

unreliable adj. Not trustworthy. Not dependable.

unromantic adj. Not romantic. This is said of someone who does not think much of love, or sentimentality.

unscrew v. Screw out. Turn around and around in order to remove.

unstable adj. Not stable. Not steady. Unbalanced. Likely to fall or break apart. "Henry's marriage has been unstable since he began drinking again."

uproariously adv. With great energy, noise and excitement.

upset v. Knock down. Cause to turn over or fall. 2. adj. Disturbed. "Milly was upset when she heard about the accident."

up-tight adj. Tense. Nervous. "Do you get up-tight when you take an exam?"

urban adj. Heavily populated, as a city. "Janet preferred to live in an urban area, while her husband preferred rural. They compromised and lived in the suburbs."

vain adj. Conceited. Proud of one's own beauty, intelligence, skill, or importance.

variant n. A variety of. A slightly different way of spelling, pronouncing a word. "Colour is the British variant of color."

vicious adj. Cruel; full of evil; very destructive. "Marcia often made vicious comments about her co-workers."

WASP n. (slang) White Anglo-Saxon Protestant. A person whose ancestors (parents, grandparents, etc.) were from England. The politically and economically dominant group in America.

whoosh v. To travel making a rushing, airy noise.

wisdom n. Intelligence and knowledge combined, with the capacity for solving problems and answering difficult questions.

Women's Liberation Movement n. A social and political effort to change the status and roles of women in society, granting them equal consideration for many types of jobs, equal pay for equal work, and the removal of stereotyped notions regarding women's nature and abilities in general.

word play n. Using words with double meanings, or similar pronunciations to cause a humorous effect.

worn-out adj. Exhausted. Tired. Used up. Full of rips or tears and holes.

yell v. Shout, scream.

BIBLIOGRAPHY

Brody, Robert--"Anatomy of a Laugh." American Health pp. 43-47. November / December, 1983.

Feinberg, Leonard--"The Secret of Humor." Maledicta, The International Journal of Verbal Aggression. Volume II, pp. 87-110. Maledicta Press, Waukesha, WI. 1978.

Nilson, Don L.F., and Alleen Pace, editors--The Language of Humor and the Humor of Language: Proceedings of the 1982 WHIM Conference.

Perret, Gene--How to Write and Sell Your Sense of Humor. Writer's Digest Books, Cincinnati, Ohio. 1982.

Peter, Dr. Laurence J., and Bill Dana--The Laughter Prescription. Ballantine Books, New York. 1982.

Wilde, Larry--How the Great Comedy Writers Create Laughter. Nelson Hall, Chicago. 1976.